FRENCH
RIVIERA

By the staff of Editions Berlitz

Berlitz Trademark Reg. U.S. Patent Office and other countries –
Marca Registrada. Library of Congress Catalog No. 78-52518.

Printed in Switzerland by Weber S.A., Bienne.

7th Printing
1984/1985 Edition

How to use our guide

- All the practical information, hints and tips that you will need before and during the trip start on page 100, with a complete rundown of contents on page 104.

- For general background, see the sections The Region and its People, p. 6, and A Brief History, p. 11.

- All the sights to see are listed between pages 20 and 77. Our own choice of sights most highly recommended is pinpointed by the Berlitz traveller symbol.

- Entertainment, nightlife and all other leisure activities are described between pages 77 and 90, while information on restaurants and cuisine is to be found on pages 91 to 99.

Although we make every effort to ensure the accuracy of all the information in this book, changes occur incessantly. We cannot therefore take responsibility for facts, prices, addresses and circumstances in general that are constantly subject to alteration. Our guides are updated on a regular basis as we reprint, and we are always grateful to readers who let us know of any errors, changes or serious omissions they come across.

Text: Suzanne Patterson
Photography: Monique Jacot
Layout: Doris Haldemann
We wish to thank Mr. and Mrs. Jean Fischbacher and Bob Davis, as well as the Société des Bains de Mer in Monte Carlo and the Caves de la Madeleine, Paris, for their help in the preparation of this guide. We're especially grateful to the tourist offices of Nice, Cannes and the Alpes Maritimes for their valuable assistance.
Cartography: Falk-Verlag, Hamburg.

4

Contents

Maps

The Region and its People

The Côte d'Azur, the Riviera, Provence, the Midi—call it what you will—this is the world's dream spot. Storied, chronicled, painted, photographed, it probably has more aura and more money than any other seacoast. It could also be called the French Gold Coast, with soaring real estate prices and cost-of-living among the world's highest.

The Riviera calls up a picture of lolling millionaires, limpid sea and pink palaces of the F. Scott Fitzgerald era. From the fabled princes or rakes gambling at Monte Carlo to lissom girls basking nude at beaches near Saint-Tropez, the

Port-Grimaud, the coast's newest little Venice, is built on canals.

coast's legends are still very real. But they are not the whole story.

The term Riviera usually includes not only the Mediterranean coast but the countryside behind, extending from around Cassis to the Italian border. The ribbons of golden sand disappearing into azure sea and the sheer, rocky spectacular views of the great Corniche routes between Nice and Monte Carlo attract obvious admiration, but less widely acclaimed sights wait to be discovered by adventurous travellers.

You can explore medieval villages—many now deserted,

or nearly so—perched perilously on their peaks, or clinging to their lofty outcrops like hazardous dice-throws. Cypresses and silvery olive groves, bright mimosa and roses, the heady wafts of thyme, rosemary and sage and the *garrigues*, the almost impenetrable scrub growth, are as much a part of southern France as the blue sea. To really savour life down here try sitting in small-town squares. Take in the musically gurgling fountains and the desultory social life under the shade of outsized plane-trees, and learn how to relax.

The sun is out twice as much here as in Paris, even if out of season the climate is not always perfect. Winter has its share of cool or cold days, and any time of year the Mistral wind can come raging down the Rhône valley freshening the vivid hues of Provence, but also exhausting inhabitants and discouraging beach-goers with its incessant, irritating roar.

Given the bright colours and pervasive, luminous light, it's no wonder that artists since Fragonard have gravitated to

Early morning—the time to beat the crowds at the Baie des Anges.

the south. Monet, Matisse, Cocteau and Picasso are just a few who celebrated the Riviera in unforgettable masterpieces.

Tourism is the area's largest business but not the only one. Other industries include ship-building, perfume, ceramics, glass and ready-to-wear garments. And the agricultural sector produces magnificent fruit and vegetables, olives, olive oil and wine for domestic consumption and for export.

Unfortunately, because of its success, this is not the place to find deserted beaches. The Riviera is thickly populated. Marseilles ranks as France's second largest city, and the number of people on the coast almost doubles in the summer.

As for the natives of Provence, they have more in common with the easy-going, voluble Italians than with their cousins to the north. They speak in a drawn-out, lilting southern-French accent. There are several dialects or *patois*, difficult for outsiders to understand.

In fact, Provençal people act much like the characters in Marcel Pagnol's novels or the cinema star Fernandel. While genial smiles prevail, there is also a good deal of eyeball-rolling, shoulder-shrugging and fist-waving. But the general mood is carefree, and you might as well sit back and forget schedules.

Just enjoy the good food and wine, the outgoing people, the beautiful scenery and sunny days that bless the French Riviera. For nowhere else will you find the marvellous blend that make this the world's most glamorous resort area.

Delights of the back country— the charming square of Saint-Paul and bright yellow hillside.

A Brief History

The attractions of the French Riviera were discovered very early on. Artefacts have been found at Beaulieu, Nice and the Grimaldi Grottoes, indicating that people lived here in Palaeolithic and Neolithic times.

More definite history begins around 1,000 B.C. with the Ligurians, far-ranging colonizers from the south east who settled along the coast. Four centuries later, the ubiquitous

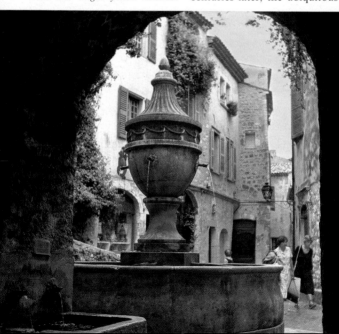

ships of Greece arrived and the Ligurians were forced to the east. These energetic Greek traders, the Phoceans, founded Marseilles, La Ciotat, Antibes and Nice. On two occasions, they called in Roman armies to help them fight the Ligurians.

Then in 125 B.C. the Romans marched in on their own account, determined to establish a passageway to their Iberian colony. They set up Provincia Narbonensis, which eventually became Provence. Among the important cities founded at this time were Narbonne, the capital, in 118 B.C., Aix in 123 B.C. and Fréjus in 49 B.C., built by Caesar as a rival to Marseilles.

The Greeks brought civilization and agriculture — the olive tree, the fig tree and grape vines — to the area; the Romans introduced their administrative systems, law and agricultural methods. Roman influence lasted for nearly six centuries; and during this period of relative peace, roads, towns and cities burgeoned all over southern France.

The Dark Ages
Christianity spread gradually throughout the Mediterranean during the first centuries A.D. In 450 the church of Provence was formally organized along

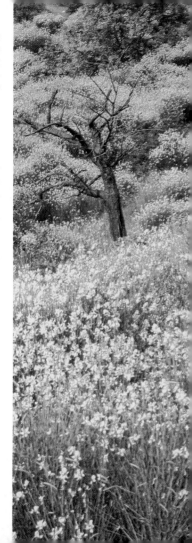

the lines of Roman administration. Then hard times followed. From the 5th to 7th centuries, successive waves of invaders swept over the country, breaking down the established order and leaving behind an utter shambles.

The Franks, who created the basis of a French state, prevailed but Provence was left more or less autonomous until the rule of Charles Martel. In several campaigns between 736 and 739 he took Avignon, Arles and Marseilles, forcefully establishing his authority over the area. Charlemagne's reign (771–814) was one of relative stability, but his heirs squabbled over the domain. In 843, the empire was divided by treaty among Charlemagne's three grandsons: Provence fell to the lot of Lothaire I. When his son Charles assumed control in 855, it became the Kingdom of Provence.

From the 8th century on, the coast was often attacked by North African Moslems, known as Moors or Saracens. In 884, they even built a mountain base at La Garde-Freinet from which they swooped down to raid and pillage neighbouring communities. Before they were driven out almost a century later by Guillaume le Libérateur, the Saracens had forced many local overlords and their followers to retreat into the hills—the origin of the perched village strongholds that dot the Midi today.

The Counts of Provence

The situation improved markedly in the 10th century. With the Saracens gone, the counts of Provence emerged as strong, independent rulers under the titular authority of the Holy Roman Empire. Trade and cultural activity revived. The 12th and 13th centuries were the heyday of the troubadours, the period when Provençal became the most important literary language of western Europe.

The counts of Barcelona gained title to Provence by a propitious marriage in 1112. One particularly able Catalonian ruler, Raimond Bérenger V, reorganized and unified the Comté of Provence. In 1246, his daughter Beatrix became the wife of Charles of Anjou (brother of Louis IX of France). The people of Provence received both commercial benefits and greater liberty from their ambitious new ruler who

La Garde-Freinet was once the base of the pillaging Saracens.

also became king of Naples and Sicily.

Avignon had its hour of glory in the 14th century. Through French influence, the bishop of Bordeaux was elected pope in 1305. The new pontiff, subservient to the kings of France, made Avignon rather than Rome his residence.

The ensuing period was a humiliating one for the Church but a golden age for Avignon. The city became a great cultural centre attracting many artists and scholars—notably Petrarch. It remained the religious capital until 1377, when Pope Gregory XI returned to Rome. But after his death, the "Great Schism" arose between Italian and French factions: there were two, and sometimes three popes (one in Avignon), each with his own College of Cardinals. The Schism did not come to an end until 1417.

Provence Becomes French

After various changes of ruling powers, the larger part of Provence (including Aix and Marseilles) came back under the control of the Dukes of Anjou. The last of them, the civic- and artistic-minded "Good King René", left his domain to his nephew, who before dying 17 months later named Louis XI, King of France, his successor. Thus Provence became part of France in 1481. Nice, however, went its separate way. It had formed an alliance with the Dukes of Savoy in 1388, and it remained Savoyard—with a few interruptions—until 1860.

Langue d'Oc

An offshoot of Latin, Provençal began to take shape in the 4th century. By the 11th, it was widely spoken in the south, carried from Nice to Bordeaux by the troubadours. These roving ambassadors went from château to château, singing the praises of idealized love. Both in style and theme, their poetry influenced the development of Western literature.

The language was known as *occitan* because *oc* rather than the northern *oïl* (which became *oui*) was the word for "yes". After the 14th century *langue d'oc* started to break down into regional dialects. Then, in 1539, Francis I decreed that French should be used in all administrative matters, and that was really the end.

Today you may hear—but certainly not understand—a bit of Niçois, Monegasque or another vestige of Provençal. Some expressions, like *lou vieux mas* (the old farmhouse), have worked themselves into everyday life.

The early 16th century was marked by strife between Francis I of France and Charles V, the Holy Roman Emperor. After an early victory in Milan (1515), the French monarch was driven out of Italy and imprisoned. Then Charles invaded Provence. In 1536, he took Aix and had himself crowned king of Arles before he was eventually checked at Marseilles and Arles and forced into a disastrous retreat.

Acting as go-between in 1538, Pope Paul III managed to get both sides to sign the Treaty of Nice, a precarious armistice at best. Never deigning to meet, each party convened separately with the pope in Nice. The truce didn't last.

In 1543, helped by the Turkish fleet, Francis I bombarded Nice (allied to his rival through the House of Savoy). After a valiant struggle, Nice repelled the invaders, returning to the realm of the House of Savoy.

Wars and Revolutions

Meanwhile Europe had become the scene of fierce religious conflicts caused by the rise of Protestantism. The confrontations were especially bloody in the south of France. In 1545 more than 20 "heretic" villages (north of Aix) were levelled by order of Francis I; the years following saw much violence on both sides. The Edict of Nantes in 1598 palliated the situation by granting religious freedom to Protestants (later revoked in 1685).

In the 17th century, Cardinal Richelieu, Louis XIII's all-powerful adviser, decided to reinforce the southern coast as protection against Spain. Toulon and Marseilles were converted into major ports. Measures of centralization and new taxes gave rise to much agitation and to outright rebellion, in the case of Marseilles. Louis XIV brought the troublesome city to heel in 1660, imposing additional contributions and restrictions.

Provence was the battleground during the 17th and 18th centuries for numerous disputes, both domestic and foreign. France took and lost Nice several times but did gain some additional territory from the Duke of Savoy. A veritable disaster hit Provence in 1720: 100,000 people died in a great epidemic that was carried into Marseilles on a ship from the Middle East.

Like the rest of France, Provence was profoundly affected by the revolution of 1789 and the cataclysmic upheavals that followed. Bad crops and the election of a new Provençal Estates General contributed to the turbulence. Riots and massacres occurred in many places.

In the administrative reorganization of France in 1790, Provence was divided into three *départements*—Var, Basses-Alpes, Bouches-du-Rhône —and violence continued.

Widespread reaction set in in 1794. Royalist extremists initiated the White Terror in Orange, Marseilles and Aix, slaughtering their Jacobin opponents. A state of lawlessness prevailed in some areas.

Man on the way up: Napoleon as portrayed by Baron Gros in 1796.

A. Held, Ecublens

Napoleon in the South

Profiting from the disarray, the English easily took Toulon in 1793. Napoleon Bonaparte, an obscure captain at the time, distinguished himself in the recapture of the city. Promoted to general, he launched his Italian campaign from Nice (annexed by France from 1793 to 1814) in 1796. Two years later, Toulon was the starting-point for his sensational Egyptian campaign. When Napoleon returned in 1799, he landed triumphantly at Saint-Raphaël. You can see a small pyramid there erected to his victories.

His empire was unpopular in Provence, where Royalist sentiment remained strong. Besides, the Continental blockade was disastrous for Marseilles' trade, further exacerbating ill-feeling.

Napoleon went through Saint-Raphaël again in 1814— but this time in disgrace, ignominiously escorted by Austrian and Russian troops on his way to exile on Elba. He escaped from his island prison a year later, landing at Golfe-Juan and returning to Paris via Cannes, Grasse, Digne and Gap—a road now known as the Route Napoléon.

The Revolution of 1848 took the form of uprisings all over the south of France, as peasants demanded land. They rebelled again in 1851 but were eventually quelled by government troops.

In 1860, the House of Savoy gave up Nice in return for Napoleon III's help in ousting the Austrians from the northern provinces of Italy. In a plebiscite, the Niçois overwhelmingly proclaimed their desire to join France. But Monaco stayed apart as a hereditary monarchy allied closely with France (see p. 41). In 1861, Monaco sold all rights to Menton and Roquebrune, which had also voted to join France.

Twentieth Century

Southern France was scarcely concerned in the First World War, and the population east of Nice felt more drawn to the Italians than anybody else. It couldn't escape the Second World War, however. In 1940, the Italians opened hostilities against France and succeeded in taking Menton. The Vichy government of Marshal Pétain was left to govern the rest of the area until the Germans took over at the end of 1942, with the Italians occupying the Côte d'Azur. But before the Germans arrived, the French scuttled their own fleet at **17**

Toulon, blocking that important harbour.

As the American, British and Allied forces approached from North Africa and Italy, the Germans put up blockhouses and barbed wire on the beaches; Saint-Tropez was dotted with mines and various beach obstacles. Then on August 15, 1944, the long-awaited landings began, led by General Patch's 7th Army. The Americans swarmed over the beach of Saint-Raphaël and destroyed the blockhouses. The following day French General de Lattre de Tassigny landed with his Free French troops at Saint-Tropez. Within two weeks Provence was free.

The scars of war were quickly erased, and with the appearance of the bikini bathing costume (a Riviera original, in spite of the name), everyone took heart. Business started to skyrocket. So did a building and tourism boom, which hasn't stopped to this day.

The Follies of Fashion

The English were the first to go to the Riviera. In the latter part of the 18th century, it was considered a fine place for consumptive and other fragile beings to escape the raw English winters. Summers, on the other hand, were shunned as being unbearably hot.

The English gravitated to Nice, especially Cimiez. Cannes was "discovered" in 1834 by Lord Brougham. Finally the French joined the sun seekers, when writers like George Sand, Alexandre Dumas and Guy de Maupassant became aware of the joys of the coast. Artists, writers, musicians, aristocrats and others followed. Every night of the winter season was brilliant with masked balls and assorted diversions.

The Riviera became a mecca for the Impressionists. Renoir and Cézanne loved the colour and light, as did the artists who arrived after them — Bonnard, Matisse, Léger and Picasso, to name but a few.

Towards the end of the 19th century, it was really the playground for international "high society", where royalty kissed the hands of American heiresses and French courtesans. The Russian aristocrats were legendary, travelling in private trains with dozens of servants.

The turn of America's affluent society came in the twenties. Charmed by the scenery and the low cost of a sybaritic life, millionaires and film stars started the vogue for the French coast in the summer.

Though the tone may have changed somewhat, people from all over still flock to the Riviera attracted by the aura of glamour and the sun.

La Croisette, a favourite rendez-vous for young and old at Cannes. **19**

Where to Go

Nice
Pop. 360,000

Nice is like a rich dowager of simple origins who never lost her common touch. Unofficial capital of the Riviera, it is a vibrant, important city, boasting France's third largest airport, an opera house and excellent philharmonic orchestra, a university and several good museums. The city's shops, hotels and restaurants rival the world's best. However, the older quarters and their inhabitants have the theatrical, good-natured, brawling character of an Italian town.

Greeks (Phoceans) from Marseilles settled here in the 4th century B.C., and the name Nice may have come from *nike*, the Greek word for victory. Two centuries later, Romans left the seaport to fishermen and built a town on the Cimiez hill.

Nice broke away from the rest of Provence in 1388, when it was annexed by the House of Savoy. In the following century, the hill now known as Le Château supported a fortified castle, and beneath it a city grew up (now the *vieille ville*).

In 1631, Nice was almost wiped out by the plague—but it survived. Bonaparte used the city as a base during his Italian campaign. It joined France officially in 1860.

Although Nice was known as a winter resort in the late 1700s, its touristic career really got underway in the next century with the arrival of the English and their queen, Victoria.

Promenade des Anglais

Any visit to Nice begins along this splendid palm-tree-lined boulevard stretching nearly 7 kilometres from just outside the airport east along the Baie des Anges to Le Château, the rock that cuts Nice off from its harbour.

The Promenade des Anglais was thus named because in 1822 the philanthropic Rev. Lewis Way encouraged the English colony to pay for the widening of a miserable footpath—creating jobs for fruit-pickers who'd been thrown out of work by a disastrous frost.

You'll pass landmarks like the legendary Negresco, an imposing hotel with a rococo façade, colourful turrets and doormen dressed in operatic costumes.

Further along on the left, you'll see a pleasant flowered

park, the **Jardin Albert-Ier**, with an 18th-century Triton fountain and a modern outdoor theatre. Behind the gardens, parallel to the Promenade des Anglais, are "shopping streets", mostly reserved for pedestrian traffic.

On the other side of the park is the Place Masséna, a picturesque square of arcaded buildings in ruddy stucco, built in 1835.

La Vieille Ville

You can enter the old city from the seaside (Quai des Etats-Unis) or the Place Masséna. From this latter direction, you'll pass the **Opéra** and its elaborate 19th-century façade. On the **Cours Saleya** (the name comes from "salt", which was at one time sold in bulk here), you shouldn't miss the afternoon flower market full of the colour and scent of roses, tulips, dahlias and geraniums. The fruit and vegetable market takes place in the morning and is just as picturesque, though more aromatic, and the open square is surrounded by cheery pizza stalls, cafés and bistros.

On the quay side, the little pastel houses where fishermen used to live (mostly restaurants and art galleries now) are known as *ponchettes*, an old provençal word meaning little

rocks. Opposite is the **Miséricorde** chapel. Built by the Black Penitents (a lay sect) in 1736, it contains an attractive altarpiece by Miralhet, *La Vierge de la Miséricorde*.

Turning left at the end of the Cours Saleya, you'll enter the old world of Nice with its appetizing aromas, tiny shops spilling their wares onto the streets, excited voices talking Niçois, a form of Provençal that rolls like Italian.

Rue Droite just looks like a cramped alleyway now, but it was the main street in the Middle Ages. On the right you'll pass the heavily decorated baroque church of Saint-Jacques, modelled after Il Gesù in Rome. Set back on the left is Sainte-Réparate cathedral (1650) with its handsome 18th-century belfry.

Showcase of the old town, the **Palais Lascaris** (15, Rue Droite) is a 17th-century town house that belonged to the Lascaris family of Ventimiglia until the French Revolution. Guided tours of historical Nice begin here. Small for a palace, the building has a handsome

A superb sampling of mollusks and crustaceans served at seafood bar.

carved marble staircase and frescoed ceilings; don't miss the odd-angled carved door, built to swing shut automatically. On the ground floor is a beautifully preserved pharmacy, dating from 1738, complete with apothecary jars. The whole shop came from Besançon, a gift of the Gould family (American industrialists).

Further on you'll find Place Saint-François with its nicely proportioned, late-baroque, former town hall. Mornings, a frenetic fish market takes over the square — gleaming with red mullet, sea bass, octopus and squid and resounding with the raucous cries of the fish merchants.

On Place Garibaldi, just outside the old town, a handsome Calder stabile stands in front of the new bus station.

Le Château and the Harbour

Though you won't find anything left of Nice's stronghold of the Middle Ages, destroyed in 1706, a visit to the 300-foot summit of Le Château is pleasant nonetheless. Hardy walkers can climb the steps in 15 minutes, but a lift service also operates from the end of the Quai des Etats-Unis. Up on top

is a public park, with exotic

Two Local Heroes

ANDRÉ MASSÉNA (1756–1817) was a late-blooming military success. Born of a wine merchant's family, he went to sea and later joined the French army. But when he left after 14 years' service, he hadn't even achieved the rank of second lieutenant. During the Revolution, Masséna re-enlisted and this time proved his mettle. Napoleon called him the "spoilt child of victory" and promoted him to Marshal of France, Duke of Rivoli and Prince of Essling. Wellington considered Masséna his most formidable rival after Napoleon. His grandson, Victor, built an elaborate mansion that now houses Nice's historical museum (see p. 78).

GIUSEPPE GARIBALDI (1807–82), hero in the struggle for Italian unification, came from Nice. He was furious when House of Savoy ceded his native city to France in 1860 in return for assistance against the Austrians. An equestrian statue of him occupies the large arcaded Place Garibaldi.

pines and cacti — and a spectacular view of the colourful port on one side and the Baie des Anges on the other. The white stones you'll see are remnants of Romanesque religious buildings. Military buffs will be interested by the naval museum in the Tour Bellenda.

Filled with pleasure and merchant boats, the port is always lively—lined with cafés and restaurants, from the simplest, rough sailors' bars to elaborate restaurants.

From the northeast corner of the harbour, you can take the Boulevard Carnot to an extraordinary new museum, the **Terra Amata,** at number 25. Practically hidden under towering residential buildings, it contains a large collection of prehistoric remains found when the land was being cleared for construction. Three hundred thousand years ago, the sea reached 85 feet higher than today, and primitive men hunted on the shores which now lie under these buildings.

Shop talk is just part of the fun on pedestrian mall in Nice.

Nice's February Lenten carnival, the famous Mardi Gras, lasts for two weeks and has its own very special personality. Begun as simple *fêtes* in the 13th century, the carnival was put on in splendid style in 1873.

Today crowds jam the boulevards, especially Place Masséna, for the parades of floats in extravagant shapes and colours. The *papier mâché* used for the floats requires about a ton of paper, plus 700 pounds of flour. Masked parades and balls alternate with the battles of flowers and confetti. The climax is the Shrove Tuesday burning of King Carnival in effigy and a sensational fireworks display, topped off by a cannon volley from the castle hill.

Cimiez

This hilly residential area—preferred first by the Romans, then by the 19th-century aristocrats—is dotted with ornate hotels resembling outdated stage sets. Queen Victoria's favourite hotel, the Régina, was the home of Matisse until his death in 1954. Now it has been divided up into flats and shops.

The way to Cimiez (you can take a bus from Place Masséna)
26 passes near the important **Chagall Museum** (see p. 78). At Cimiez itself, the brick ruins of the entry to the Roman arena area are a rendezvous for young mothers and their charges.

The Villa des Arènes houses two rather dusty-looking museums. Rush through the archaeological museum (unless that subject is your passion) and enjoy the **Matisse museum** at leisure; it's a collection of the master's works, from sketches to monumental collages, including mementoes like his palette and an old shell-shaped chair from his studio.

Behind the villa, for a small fee, you can walk around the Roman ruins (2nd and 3rd centuries A.D.) which look like rubble until brought to life by a guide. The 33-foot-high walls were the *frigidarium* (cold) part of the Roman bath complex, fed by fresh streams and undoubtedly fancier than any modern sauna.

The nearby Cimiez Franciscan church is a heavy, 19th-century "Gothic" construction containing three remarkable paintings on wood by the Bréa brothers, 15th-century Niçois painters.

Nice Excursions

Nice is an excellent starting point for short tours all along the Riviera and for some out-

Wriggling whitebait fresh from the sea; below: the imposing ruins of Roman baths at Cimiez.

of-the-ordinary trips into the area behind Nice.

If you like mountain views—and are not frightened by mountain driving—take the Beuil-Valberg circuit, a daylong tour featuring the **Gorges du Cians.** Flowing down 5,250 feet to the Var, the River Cians cuts through awesome chasms of grey and red limestone rock. The road is sometimes lined with icicle walls. Stops include the old alpine town of BEUIL, the modern ski resort of VALBERG and the old fortified town of ENTREVAUX, with a Gothic church and 17th-century altarpiece.

Another spectacular excursion goes to the **Vésubie Valley**—green mountain slopes and rushing waters fed by melting snows. Make sure to visit the town of SAINT-MARTIN-VÉSUBIE, located on a spur between two torrential streams—the Boréon and the Madone de Fenestre—that form the Vésubie. In summer, it's a headquarters for mountain climbers.

The sinuous road leading up to the **Madone d'Utelle** (3,850 feet) passes by an interesting 18th-century church in UTELLE. At the summit you'll find a breathtaking view and a sanctuary founded in 850 (rebuilt in 1806).

The Corniches

The pre-Alpine mountains between Nice and Menton drop to the sea in a changing panorama of spectacular scenery.

Highest views are from the route known as the **Grande Corniche,** built by Napoleon along the ancient Aurelian Way. The **Moyenne** (middle) **Corniche** offers a contrast of rocky cliffs and the sea. The **Corniche Inférieure,** or Corniche du Littoral, runs along beside the sea and can be terribly crowded in summer but some very worthwhile places are located on this road.

Six kilometres east of Nice, **Villefranche** is one of the most sheltered Mediterranean harbours, quieter since the U.S. Navy stopped using it as a base.

Clinging to a steep slope under the road, Villefranche offers instant charm, with its yellow, pink and red stucco or brick houses packed against the hill, the plunging alleyways and staircases and the covered **Rue Obscure** that snakes down to the sea. The quayside cafés are well placed for watching the pleasure boats and for a

The colourful Villefranche quay is fine for fishing or a picnic.

28

view of Cap Ferrat, pointing off to the left like a green finger.

On the right, below the town's old citadel (built for the Duke of Savoy in 1560), is the 14th-century Chapelle Saint-Pierre, also known as the **Cocteau chapel,** since writer-artist Jean Cocteau decorated it in 1956. The pastel, boldly outlined drawings completely fill the small vaulted chapel with scenes of fishermen, plus biblical episodes from the life of St. Peter.

A short drive around the rocky, pine-green peninsula of **Cap Ferrat** will convince you that the rich indeed appreciate privacy. The view is mostly of gates with hints of grandeur behind them. The vast, cream-coloured villa that belonged to King Leopold II of the Belgians can only be seen from afar. Somerset Maugham lived in Villa Mauresque, also rather well hidden.

The best views are from the upper levels of the **Ephrussi de Rothschild** foundation, also known as Musée Ile-de-France. Built in 1905–12 by Madame Béatrice Ephrussi, née Roth-schild, the pinkish Italian-style villa is the delirious assemblage of an insatiable art collector. While you'll see a Coromandel screen and other beautiful *chi-noiseries*, plus examples of Renaissance, Louis XIII furniture and a few Impressionist paintings, the museum really shines in its French 18th-century pieces. The collection of Sèvres porcelain, composed of thousands of rare pieces and signed complete sets, is perhaps the largest in the world. The museum opens only in the afternoon and closes Mondays.

The gardens surrounding the villa are no less extraordinary: the main one is French style, but bordered by others of worldwide inspiration.

Not far away, the modest Cap Ferrat zoo offers an unlikely contrast. Favourite with children are the trained monkey shows *(Ecole des chimpanzés)*.

SAINT-JEAN-CAP-FERRAT is the port side of the peninsula, with a modern seaside promenade and an older fishing village; Cocteau decorated the marriage room of its small town hall.

The main thing to see in the small resort of BEAULIEU is the Villa Kérylos, a monument to the glory of Greece built at the turn of the century by scholar-musician-bibliophile Théodore Reinach.

Reinach studied and planned for years, all the while collecting artefacts. Then he commissioned an Italian architect, Pontremoli, to design a Greek mansion that would be perfect in every detail. Built out of cool marble and fruitwood, the house has a pleasant peristyle courtyard in Carrara marble and a "study" of grandiose proportions with mosaic floors. So as not to ruin the effect, Reinach even hid his upright piano behind a Greek-looking console. It is said the fanatic Graecophile occasionally dined with family and friends reclining on high couches.

Ephrussi de Rothschild museum, a pink palace on Cap Ferrat.

The Grande Corniche road goes all the way to Menton (via Roquebrune and the Vistaëro lookout). You can stop off at La Turbie, or explore the higher roads, visiting villages like PEILLE and PEILLON.

On a clear day, the **Belvédère d'Eze** (1,680 ft.) offers a panoramic view of the coast, the Tête de Chien mountain over Monte Carlo, the old perched city of Eze below and, on the right, as far as Cap d'Antibes and the Estérel mountains.

LA TURBIE's star curiosity is the **Trophée des Alpes,** a round ruin with Doric columns standing guard over Monaco. Emperor Augustus built it in 6 B.C. to celebrate victory over various battling peoples who had prevented the construction of a road between Rome and Gaul. Blown up and used as a quarry at various times, the mutilated monument has been partially restored.

Highlight off the Moyenne Corniche (best road of the three) is the village of **Eze.** It hangs at a dizzying angle above the sea—majestic and deep blue from this perspective. One of the most magnificent views on the coast.

The medieval town is closed to traffic but not tourists, who flock here in all seasons. On the site of an old château, razed in 1706 by Louis XIV, you'll find a public garden full of exotic flowers and cacti. Amble around the narrow stone streets, fully equipped with souvenir shops.

Continuing on, the Moyenne Corniche skirts around Mo-

CORNICHES

aco (see p. 37). Enjoy the stunning view at CABBÉ before turning off for Roquebrune and Menton.

Instead of **Roquebrune** ("brown rock"), the town should really have been called 'Roquerose'—for pink is what you see here on a sunny day (caused by reflections from the sienna-red stucco buildings along the narrow streets).

You can visit the dungeon of the fortified castle, built in the 10th century by a count of Ventimiglia to fend off the Saracens. Stony and spartan, the ruin still looks very much the fortress, with walls 6 to 12 feet thick and a bedroom furnished with a blunderbuss. A hole plunging hundreds of feet down was just what it looks like—a toilet!

Part of the Roquebrune municipality, the CAP MARTIN promontory is a millionaire's enclave, green with pine and olive trees, favoured in the last century when nobody cared much for sea-bathing (there is no beach).

Hot-point of the Riviera for climate, lukewarm for fun and games, **Menton** is a favourite

Witness to the past: a narrow medieval street in Roquebrune.

of retired people for its warmth, simplicity and two casinos (the main one is a baroque gem).

Lemons flourish in this sunny spot. In February, they even hold a lemon festival—the 15 or so tons of citrus fruits used in the décor are later sent to hospitals or made into jam. Menton is also proud of its olives and *clémentines* (a type of tangerine). It's no surprise that the natives like to tell their Adam-and-Eve legend: when they were chased from Paradise, Eve took along a lemon. After finding this new garden very like Paradise, she planted the "immortal fruit" which sprang up all over the slopes under the greyish limestone mountains.

A long pebble beach and Promenade George V lead to a 16th-century bastion, now a **Cocteau museum;** further along is a jetty with a lighthouse and the modern Garavan harbour. You can see how the old town crowds up from the sea.

After a stop at the **Place aux Herbes,** with its arcades and three huge plane trees, you go uphill to reach the heart of the **old town.** It has a decidedly

Happily dozing in its sun-warmed setting, Menton attracts young yachtsmen and seasoned sailors.

Italian air. Here the 17th-century church of **Saint-Michel** occupies a charming square with a view right to Italy.

Cocteau painted some bold and fanciful allegorical frescoes in the marriage room of the Hôtel de Ville (town hall). The Musée Municipal contains odd bits of folklore, modern works and old bones, though not the famed pre-historic Grimaldi man once exhibited here.

Two public gardens in Menton are worth a look. The

Rocky hike around Sainte-Agnès, highest of the perched villages.

Jardin Botanique, arranged around a villa called Val Rahmeh, proves that everything can indeed grow in Menton—from a riot of roses to Mexican yucca, fuchsia and Japanese cane bamboo. More curious is the **Jardin des Colombières.** Built by writer-painter Ferdinand Bac, the Hellenic-style villa (now a modest hotel-restaurant) sits in the midst of Mediterranean lushness—with a splendid view. The terraced gardens out back are a romantic haven of flowered walks, punctuated by cypresses, ponds, fountains and statuary.

Around Menton, hikers can venture up through groves of gnarled olive trees, pine and scrub oak and finally the thick *maquis,* or bushy growth, scented with wild herbs.

Picturesque sites just a short drive away include L'ANNONCIADE, a Capuchin monastery with a beautiful view; SAINTE-AGNÈS, which claims to be the highest of the local perched villages; and the picturesque medieval towns of GORBIO and CASTELLAR.

If you long for real Italian spaghetti, just cross the border to **Ventimiglia.** A visit here should include the Romanesque cathedral, the baptistery (11th century) and a walk through the old streets.

Monaco

Pop. 23,500

This fairytale princedom, an enclave rising from the rocks above the sea, is famed for its casino and wealth. Monaco owes much of its current success to dashing Prince Rainier and to the charm of the late Princess Grace.

The atmosphere here is both big city and miniature operatic. There are crowds in this paradise, with a population density comparable to Hong Kong's and cars jamming thoroughfares all over the hills (strolling is for the sturdy). But the smartly uniformed Monegasque *gendarmes* keep order, and the streets are the cleanest on the Riviera.

Don't get the idea that gambling is the only local attraction; a mere 5 per cent of the principality's revenue comes from the casino. Many other commercial and cultural activities take precedence. For one thing, Monaco is a music capital with a top European orchestra, an opera house and a music festival. Then there's the motor rally and the Grand Prix, synonymous with the name Monte Carlo, which set the sinuous streets roaring. Besides brilliant galas and balls, Monaco holds a dog show, **37** flower show and TV festival. It also boasts a good soccer team and a radio station that beams all over Europe. Last but not least, philatelists know Monaco's beautiful stamps.

To clarify nomenclature: Monaco refers to the principality, geographically the historic peninsula-rock where you'll see the palace; Monte Carlo (which means Mount Charles) is the newer 19th-century area curving out east of the rock. In between lies La Condamine, a land-fill flat area, comprising the harbour and modern business district.

Monte Carlo

All roads lead to the main **casino** (and opera), introduced by a neatly tended garden-promenade. Any resemblance to the Paris Opéra is more than coincidental, since architect Charles Garnier designed both.

A busily decorated foyer with frescoes and bosomy caryatides in 19th-century style take you in to the opera. Off to the left are the gambling rooms. If you can tear your eyes away from the roulette wheels, the ornate décor here is a delight. Especially amusing is the Salon Rose, where painted, unclad nymphs float about the ceiling smoking **38** cigarillos.

Next door stands the **Hôtel de Paris,** an equally opulent historical monument. Louis XIV's bronze horse in the entrance hall has so often been "stroked for luck" by gamblers that its extended fetlock shines like gold. The dining room on the right is an impressive though somewhat gloomy example of the heavy style of the Second Empire. The great chef Escoffier created dishes here for his celebrated clients.

Across the square, you'll find the lively Café de Paris, a crowded rendez-vous that hums with the frantic whir of slot machines, helpfully installed for the use of gambling addicts between drinks.

Nearby, Monaco's **National Museum** contains a delightful doll museum! Also known as the Musée Galéa, this whimsical spot houses a 2,000-piece collection assembled by Madeleine de Galéa. The villa-museum designed by Charles Garnier is a pink confection, perfect as a doll's house, nestled in a garden that has statues by Rodin, Maillol and Bourdelle. Exhibits include tableaux and exquisitely outfitted dolls from the 18th century to modern

Monte Carlo's star attraction—its baroque casino-opera house.

models. A series of automatons perform when the guard winds them up; there are extraordinary "acts" by mechanical card-players, acrobats, dancers and a snake-charmer — slightly spooky but quite impressive. Children love it.

The Monaco Rock

A short ride up the hill from the centre of town, you'll find the **Palais du Prince** (bus or taxi recommended; parking space is severely limited).

The Grimaldis still live here, so you can only go inside while they're on holiday (July and August). The summer tour includes a look at the magnificent 17th-century interior courtyard with its double marble staircase and painted gallery **(Galerie d'Hercule).** There are several well-maintained rooms containing priceless antiques, a gallery of mirrors, paintings by Van Loo, Brueghel and Titian, royal family portraits and the elaborate bed where the Duke of York died in 1767.

Any time of the year, at 11.55 a.m., you can watch the changing of the guard outside the palace. With fife and drums, much circumstance and little pomp, it's a good five minutes' worth of entertainment — though hardly up to Buckingham Palace standards.

The Grimaldis

Monaco's past is sensational —full of intrigues and murder in high places. By a tortuous path, it arrived at the present constitutional monarchy under the personal rule of Prince Rainier III.

The rock of Monaco was inhabited from the Stone Age onwards. In 1215, the Genoese built a fortress there, which the Guelf and Ghibelline factions disputed for the rest of the century. Finally in 1297, the Guelfs led by François Grimaldi gained the upper hand. The Grimaldi family has hung on tenaciously ever since.

Treaties with powerful neighbours assured Monaco's independence over the years (except for a French interlude from 1793 to 1814). Roquebrune and Menton broke off from the principality in 1848 and were later bought by France. Looking for a new source of revenue, Monaco's ruler, Charles III, founded the Société des Bains de Mer in 1861 to operate gambling facilities. The venture got off to a slow start, but when François Blanc, a financial and administrative wizard with a shady background, took over, business prospered. On Blanc's advice, Charles commissioned the construction of a casino and opera house.

Hotels went up, and a railway line from the rest of the coast was soon extended to Monaco. A new (though perilous) coach-road and word-of-mouth publicity brought gamblers and fun-seekers.

In spite of tricky legal tangles, Monaco has retained its independent (and tax-free!) status, with open boundaries to France, free currency exchange (French money is almost always used) and a common post-telephone system with France.

Monaco is a nice place to live but it's almost impossible to become a citizen—unless you can find some Monegasque ancestors.

The **old town** is also located on the Monaco Rock. Along the narrow pedestrian streets riddled with souvenir shops, restaurants and other tourist attractions, a gay atmosphere prevails, ringing with the Italian inflections of Monegasque *patois*.

On Rue Basse, you'll come across **L'Historial des Princes de Monaco**—a quaint wax museum assembled in 1971 by a Frenchman who likes Monaco. From the earliest Grimaldi, François, to the youngest, Princess Stéphanie, the beautifully costumed personages present a pleasant historical panorama.

The cathedral is a white, 19th-century neo-Romanesque monster, boasting a tryptich by Louis Bréa (right transept).

The **Musée Océanographique,** a formidable, grey-pillared construction, was founded in 1910 by Prince Albert I, who spent the better part of his time at sea. Most expensive museum to visit on the coast, it is now directed by Commandant Jacques-Yves Cousteau, the underwater explorer. In the basement aquarium, playful sea lions, jaded turtles, staring grouper fish and thousands of small incandescent fish cavort, delighting adults and children.

The cliff-hanging **Jardin Exotique** above the Condamine is worth visiting for the good view of the principality and environs. A series of stepping stones leads you through a display of exotic plants—especially fierce-looking spiny cacti in thousands of varieties, from South America and Africa.

Near the entrance is the **Anthropological Museum** (*Musée d'Anthropologie Préhistorique*), where you'll see old bones from Menton and Monaco caves, plus ancient jewellery found in the Condamine. The 250 steps down to the *grottes* will reward you with a cool promenade through lacy

Monaco is both a bustling high-rise city and a seaside resort.

pinpoints of stalactites and stalagmites; but you have to walk up again to get out!

Not far off is a zoo — small, friendly but unspectacular except for a good view.

Nice to Cannes

In all respects, this is one of the richest areas of the Riviera. The scenery can be magnificent, and art works abound both along the coast and in the villages behind.

Côte d'Antibes

Founded by the Phoceans in the 4th century B.C., **Antibes** got its name (Antipolis — the "city opposite") because it faced Nice across the Baie des Anges. The first landmark you'll see here is the imposing square fortress, **Fort Carré.** This was the French kings' stronghold against the dukes of Savoy who controlled Nice.

In 1794, Napoleon lodged his family here while supervising the coastal defence. Since he wasn't very well paid, his mother had to do her own laundry, and his sisters filched figs and artichokes from neighbouring farmers. Today the hills around Antibes are lined with glassy greenhouses; growing flowers is the main local industry.

Don't miss a tour around the ramparts, reconstructed by Vauban in the 17th century along the original medieval lines. The **Château Grimaldi,** now the Musée Picasso, is a white stone castle with a Romanesque tower built by the lords of Antibes on a Roman site. Besides many classical relics, the museum possesses a rich Picasso collection. In 1946, when the artist was having difficulty finding a place to work, the director of Antibes' museum offered him the premises as a studio. Picasso set to work among the dusty antiquities. Inspired by the classical objects around him, he completed over 145 works in a period of six months. The grateful artist gave these drawings, ceramics, paintings and other pieces from a later period to the museum.

Next to the château-museum is a 17th-century **church** with a Romanesque apse and transept and an altarpiece attributed to Louis Bréa. Behind the sunny square you'll find a maze of old streets and the covered market, colourful in the morning when it's in full swing.

Just around the bay lies the **Cap d'Antibes,** a quiet, pine-covered peninsula well endowed with big, beautiful

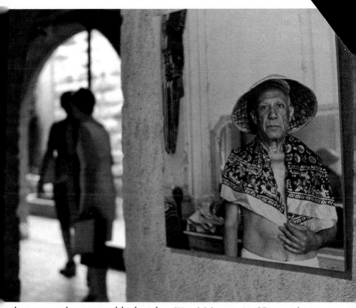

Watchful portrait of Picasso hangs in museum among his own works.

houses and a venerable hotel, the Eden-Roc. It served as a model for F. Scott Fitzgerald, and today you can usually see film stars and magnates lolling around its pool poised high above the sea.

The **Chapelle Notre-Dame** at LA GAROUPE is of curious composition: one nave is 13th century, the other 16th, and each is dedicated to a different madonna. They are both filled with ex-votos, all kinds of naïve art works or objects offered as prayers of thanks. Around the western side of the cape is the sandy crescent-shaped bay of JUAN-LES-PINS. The resort enjoyed its heyday in the twenties and thirties after American tycoon Frank Jay Gould built a big hotel and casino in a pinewood setting. Sleepy in winter, the town becomes rather wild in summer with a **45**

mosphere generated by
... s, cafés, boutiques
... heir wares into the
... ets and a restless, fun-
seeking crowd of young people.

The artisans' towns of Vallauris and Biot are only a few
minutes' drive from Antibes.
Vallauris is inevitably associa-
ted with Picasso, who worked
here after the war, giving
new impetus to a dying ceramics and pottery industry.
He presented the town with the
bronze statue, *Man with a
Sheep*, on Place Paul-Isnard
and decorated the Romanesque
chapel there with his monumental **murals** *War and Peace*
(1952–59).

Careful buyers still find
worthwhile purchases in the
ceramics shops that line Vallauris' one main street.

Perched on a cone-shaped
hill, **Biot** also bulges with
artisans' shops and has a restored Romanesque church
(too dark most of the time to
see a fine Bréa altarpiece) and
a colourful 13th-century square
with fountains and arcades.

Downhill, in the Biot glass-
works you can see craftsmen
dressed in shorts fashioning the
heavy, tinted glass with minute
bubbles that the town is known
for.

Adjacent to Biot, the **Musée
National Fernand Léger** with

its bold façade stands out like a giant postage stamp from miles away. Light and airy, the modern structure, built and donated to France by the artist's widow, houses an incomparable collection of Léger's works — from paintings to enormous tapestries.

Children like the dolphin show at Marineland near Biot railway station, while food buffs will be interested in the gastronomic museum at VILLENEUVE-LOUBET, the birthplace of chef Auguste Escoffier.

Inland Route

Spread out over hills covered with orange and olive trees,

CAGNES-SUR-MER is not one but three towns: the seaside resort of CROS-DE-CAGNES, the modern commercial section of LE LOGIS and the ancient hilltop fortress, **Haut-de-Cagnes** — the prettiest and most interesting part. Its narrow, cobbled streets corkscrew up to the **castle**. To enter, you pass through an ivy-covered, oblique-angled patio with galleries all around and a huge pepper tree in the centre. On the ground floor of the castle visit a curious museum devoted to olives — their history, cultivation, literature — probably the greatest tribute ever paid to that fruit.

Upstairs are exhibits of con-

TOULON – NICE

temporary art and a ceremonial hall with a 17th-century *trompe-l'œil* ceiling, *The Fall of Phaeton*. One extraordinary room contains 40 portraits of Suzy Solidor, the one-time cabaret queen, as seen by famous 20th-century painters—from a doe-eyed girl wearing a sailor suit by Van Dongen to a raffish, much older version of her wearing a matador's hat.

Renoir spent his last years (1907–19) in the villa of Les Collettes just east of Cagnes. However, there's not much left to see here besides mementoes and a few of the master's minor works.

Saint-Paul-de-Vence is another venerable bastion, built within spade-shaped walls and looming over green terraces of vineyards, bougainvillea, mimosa and cypress—plus lots of recently built villas.

The walled feudal city, entered by foot under a tower and arch with a cannon pointing right at you, was built by Francis I in the 16th century as a defence against Nice and the dukes of Savoy.

Under the big plane trees of the Place du Général-de-Gaulle, you'll usually find a

Special sights on Côte d'Azur—a stunning sunrise and potter at work in artisan town of Vallauris.

lively game of *pétanque* (or *boules*), the outdoor bowling game played with leaded balls. The Colombe d'Or restaurant across the street has an important collection of modern painting—Matisse, Derain, Dufy, Utrillo among others—assembled by the owner's father.

You can make the tour of the narrow pedestrian streets in a few minutes or at a leisurely pace with stops at the Grande Fontaine and a look at the Gothic church.

On a grassy hill just outside Saint-Paul is one of the great modern art museums of the world—the **Fondation Maeght,** inaugurated in 1964 by Paris art dealer Aimé Maeght and his wife. The museum sits in a green grove of dark pines. Full of visual surprises, the brick-steel-glass construction designed by Spanish-American architect José Luis Sert is an ideal place for exploring modern art. Heralded by a black Calder stabile at the entry, the works inside include ceramics by Miró, bronze filament-figures by Giacometti, fountains and stained-glass windows by Braque—to say nothing of the paintings and lithographs by many of the great names of 20th-century art.

Vence is an ancient bishopric 49

with middle-age spread: the charming old city has been girdled by newer shops and houses. English and French artists and retired people like the bustling atmosphere, the fragrant surrounding hills and the peace that falls at night (off-season, of course!).

In the 17th century, the remarkable Antoine Godeau became bishop of Vence. A misshapen society wit, he turned to the holy orders at the age of 30, undertook restoration of the cathedral, founded new industries to give work to his parishioners and was appointed one of the first members of the august Académie Française.

Best scenic points of old Vence are the **Place du Peyra** with its gurgling fountain and friendly cafés, the cathedral (especially the arresting Romanesque belfry), and the **Place**

A ramble through the old town of Tourrettes is always rewarding; opposite: Grasse flower market.

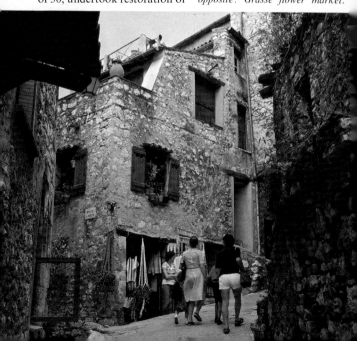

du Frêne with a centuries-old ash tree whose trunk must be at least 6 feet in diameter.

Tourists often hurry past Vence on their way to the **Chapelle du Rosaire-Henri Matisse** on the road to Saint-Jeannet (open October–May on Tuesdays and Thursdays, 10–11.30 a.m. and May–September every day 4–5 p.m.). Dedicated by Matisse to the Dominican nuns who cared for him during a long illness, the chapel is the crowning achievement of the artist, then in his eighties and practically blind. The famed stained-glass windows in bold patterns of royal blue, bright green and yellow give radiant light to the simple chapel, two walls of which are decorated by powerful line-drawing figures on white faience.

A short tour of the **Loup Valley** is worthwhile and will take you less than a day. Highlights include Tourrettes, a charming old town popular with artisans and artists, several waterfalls (Cascade de Courmes, Cascade des Demoiselles) and the town of Gourdon, built on a steep spur 2,500 feet high. The castle here was a Saracen fort in the 9th century and contains a small medieval museum.

Grasse, the world's perfume capital, won't knock you over

with heady scents; but you can't miss the enormous signs inviting you to visit the factories.

Although the Grassois were distilling essential essences from local flowers as far back as the 13th century, the industry didn't bloom until the Medici family launched the fashion of scented gloves in the **51**

16th century (Grasse made gloves as well).

Nowadays the manufacturers use at least 10,000 tons of flowers—violets (January to March), mimosa (February), daffodil (April), rose and orange-flowers and so on—to produce their essence. The gleaming brass cauldrons, alembics and other trappings displayed in the factories, though mainly for show, do give an idea of the first steps in making perfume and soap.

The high price of perfume becomes understandable when you realize it takes a ton of petals to produce 2.2 pounds of essence. The attractive soaps and scents on sale here have little to do with the sophisticated Paris-made brands, which use Grasse essences in secret formulas.

Built on a steep hill, Grasse was already renowned for its good air in the 19th century, and invalids and people on holiday flocked here. The most

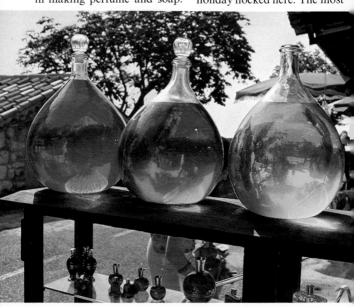

charming spot in town is the friendly, crowded **Place aux Aires,** with its fountains, arcades and sculptured 18th-century façades. The morning market is a palette of brilliant colours (flowers and vegetables) under the blue shade of lotus *(micocoulier)* and plane trees.

A few blocks downhill, the Place aux Herbes has an even larger food market. Several steps away is the sober, ochre-stone **cathedral,** begun in the 12th century and restored in the 17th. Inside you'll find cradle-vaulting and a rare religious canvas by Honoré Fragonard, *The Washing of the Feet.*

The **Musée Fragonard,** just off Cours Honoré-Cresp, is an elegant 18th-century town house, with rooms of admirable proportions, a hall and stairway in *trompe-l'œil.* It originally belonged to the Marquise de Cabris. Fragonard stayed here in 1790, fleeing the Revolution in Paris. He brought with him a series of love-scene paintings which had been turned down by Madame du Barry. Most of the collection has ended up in the Frick

Perfumes come in many hues at Gourdon; right: a cool sail on artificial lake of Saint-Cassien.

Museum in New York, but the excellent, sensuous *Three Graces* remains.

The Marquise de Cabris' furniture is in remarkably good condition. Among the less conventional articles on display are a nicely carved wooden bidet-chair with shell-shaped basin and a pewter bathtub on wheels.

Grasse is a good starting point for delightful side trips. Gourdon and the Loup Valley (see p. 51) are off to the northeast; to the south-west you have the Tanneron range and the man-made lake of Saint-Cassien.

CABRIS (6 km. on the D4 road) commands an impressive view from its old château ruins — the Tanneron hills, the Esterel and La Napoule to the right, Mougins and the Lérins Islands to the left; and on a clear day you can even make out the hazy outline of Corsica.

Another 8 kilometres or so further on, the GROTTES DE SAINT-CÉZAIRE provide refreshing respite from the sun with stalactite shapes in extraordinary dark-red and pink colours. SAINT-CÉZAIRE itself is a peaceful, pretty town with a Romanesque chapel and a good view. You can continue north through wild, rocky limestone hills with low trees and bushes, up to MONS (32 km. from Grasse), an ancient perched village, to the COL DE VAL-FERRIÈRE, and back down the Route Napoléon through SAINT-VALLIER and several splendid panoramas.

Or you may want to continue west into the Var, visiting typical towns like FAYENCE (27 km. from Grasse), BARGEMON (44 km.), DRAGUIGNAN (56 km.) and perhaps the **Abbaye du Thoronet** (two hours' drive from Grasse). Lost in a beautiful landscape of reddish bauxite and green pine scrub trees, it's a cool, quiet place. The pink-stoned Thoronet, one of the three great abbeys of Provence, dates from the 12th century. It is notable for its clean-lined simplicity, its squat, colonnaded cloister and a hexagonal fountain, the *lavabo*, where the monks used to bathe.

Cannes
Pop. 68,000

During the film festival in May and the record festival (MIDEM) in January, Cannes loses its habitual cool. The rest of the year the city devotes itself to its touristic vocation — as an elegant, cosmopolitan resort in a beautiful setting, with the liveliest pleasure port on the Riviera.

The history of Cannes is linked to the two islands you can see off the coast, the Lérins. On the smaller one, St. Honorat founded a monastery in the 4th century which became a famous shrine for pilgrims. In the 10th century the Count of Antibes gave the Cannes mainland to the Lérins monks. They built ramparts to defend the lands against incursions by Moorish pirates.

By 1788, only four monks remained; the monastery was closed down and Cannes came under French rule. In 1815, Napoleon stopped there after landing at Golfe-Juan. But Cannes gave him a chilly reception; he had to move on to Grasse.

Like Nice's Promenade des Anglais, the **Croisette** is a magnificent showcase with gleaming hotels lining a flowered boulevard. The golden sand of the beach along the promenade is mainly imported from Fréjus. At one end of the Croisette lies the old port and the new **Palais des Festivals;** at the other, a second port and the Palm Beach Casino. The film festival plus multiple other festivities are held in the grand new Palais, which contains a casino as well.

Just a few blocks behind the

Cannes is "Discovered"

Cannes was just a quiet fishing village in 1834, when Lord Brougham, a leading English law reformer, had to stop over on his way to Italy because of a cholera epidemic. This chance visit turned out to be longer than expected: he built a home and returned every winter for the rest of his life.

A champion of his adopted city, Lord Brougham prodded King Louis-Philippe to provide funds for a jetty below the old town. Many English aristocrats followed Brougham to Cannes, as tourists and settlers, swelling the local population. A handsome statue of Lord Brougham, the man who "discovered" the town, presides over Prosper Mérimée Square, just across from the Palais des Festivals.

Cannes Film Festival—a field day for cinema fans and fanciers.

Croisette is the **Rue d'Antibes,** one of the coast's most glamorous shopping streets. For more down-to-earth wares—like tee-shirts, sandals, mouth-watering sausages and pastries—head for Rue Meynadier.

Looking uphill from the old port in the evening, you have a vision of the ramparts of the old town, **Le Suquet,** glowing with orange lights against the dark purple sky. You'll also see the **Tour du Suquet,** a 72-foot-high square watchtower built by the Lérins monks. It was destroyed during the Revolution, but later restored, as a favour to local fishermen who petitioned for a tall, visible navigational point. Now the white stone clock tower is a Cannes trademark.

The centre of the old town is Place de la Castre (from the Latin word for castle), a quiet, pine-shaded square. The 17th-century "Gothic" church here, rather dim inside, has several polychrome statues.

The **Musée de la Castre** (closed on Mondays) houses a quaintly eclectic assemblage of everything from an Egyptian mummy's hand to a Japanese warrior's costume and a South Pacific hut pole. The Persian objects are quite good. The donor of all this, a Dutchman named Baron Lycklama, is portrayed in an extraordinary Oriental outfit.

The view over Cannes from Le Suquet is superb. For an even more spectacular panorama, go to the **observatory** at Super-Cannes.

Iles de Lérins

One of Cannes' most refreshing diversions is an excursion to the islands. Boats leave frequently in the summer: the trip to Sainte-Marguerite takes about 15 minutes; to Saint-Honorat, 30. In season, they hold sound-and-light shows.

About a mile and a half of wooded hills, a minute "main" street lined with fishermen's houses and a couple of restaurants, **Sainte-Marguerite** is the closer and larger island. It takes its name from St. Honorat's sister who founded her own religious order.

Walk uphill to visit the old **Fort Royal,** built under Cardinal Richelieu, and enjoy a

58 marvellous view of Cannes,

Antibes and the hills. The main attraction here is the dank and smelly prison of the "Man in the Iron Mask". There's nothing to see but chains, faded ochre stone and modern graffiti, but the legend is intriguing.

Between 1687 and 1698 a masked prisoner was kept here. Actually his mask was of cloth, not iron, but he wore it constantly and nobody knows for sure who he was or why he was imprisoned. One theory identifies him as an illegitimate brother of Louis XIV; another as the larcenous ex-finance minister Fouquet.

On Sainte-Marguerite you can walk for hours among cool, fragrant woods and a grove of enormous eucalyptus trees, a Riviera staple that was first brought to the coast from Australia in the early 19th century.

The island of **Saint-Honorat,** home of the monks who governed Cannes for nearly eight centuries, is once again a monastery, run by the Cistercian Order.

Bright green and gentle with umbrella pines, roses, lavender and the monks' vineyard, it's a peaceful retreat in the off-season. Wandering around you'll come upon several small Romanesque barrel-vaulted chapels.

The most striking construction is the square, battlemented **"château"** — really a fortified dungeon. Built in the 11th century over a Roman cistern, it served as a refuge for the monks during various attacks.

The 19th-century monastery is only open for special visits on request. However, you can see the small museum and church, accompanied by a guide. Next door to the museum the monks do a brisk trade in handicrafts, lavender scent and their own liqueur — a redoubtable-looking yellowish liquid.

Around Cannes

The coast's most glorious oddity, the **Château de la Napoule** (8 km. west of Cannes), hovers in red-rock splendour over a coin-sized beach and harbour.

Here, in 1919 American sculptor Henry Clews (scion of a New York banking family) restored the medieval château with towers and battlements, endowing every possible inch with his own work. Wildly imaginative, the sculptures range from a poignant Don Quixote to pudgy grotesques of African inspiration.

The eccentric Clews, who saw himself as a latter-day Quixote and his wife as "the Virgin of La Mancha", filled his home with mottoes, ridiculing the "aberrations" of society.

The museum hours are almost as quixotic as the décor, though you can usually get in in the afternoon, except for Saturday and Sunday.

A soft and subtle backdrop of green hills characterizes the countryside between Cannes and Grasse, the *arrière-pays*.

Interesting stops include MOUGINS, a 15th-century fortified town (with a few superb restaurants); VALBONNE, with its beautiful arcaded square shaded by big elms and a brightly restored Romanesque church; and PLASCASSIER, a sleepy village on a hill.

The Esterel

Between Cannes and Saint-Raphaël lie a mass of porphyry rocks worn down and chipped by streams. This is the Esterel, now not much more than 2,000 feet at its highest, though the landscape seems abrupt and impressive. In the spring, the scrub-herb hills are golden with mimosa.

The original inland road through the Esterel was the Aurelian Way, built by the Roman emperor in the 3rd century.

These days, most people take the Côte d'Azur motorway be- **59** tween Cannes and Saint-Raphaël, but the coastal route — the **Corniche d'Or** (the Golden Corniche) — is certainly prettier. Reddish porphyry rocks tumble into the dark blue sea making a jigsaw pattern of colours and shapes, tempting you to stop at every outcrop to admire the view.

After LA NAPOULE and then THÉOULE, with its "château" that served as a soap factory in the 18th century, you come to PORT-LA-GALÈRE, a cascade of modern houses on a flowered stony point. The Esterel is full of little fishing ports with euphonic names — LE TRAYAS, ANTHÉOR, AGAY. The **Sémaphore du Dramont,** built on the ruins of a watch-tower, offers sweeping views of the coast, and near the road is a marble monument commemorating the American landing here on August 15, 1944.

The best time to see this coast is at sunset looking east, when colours and contrasts are most flamboyant, a surrealist's dream.

Saint-Raphaël

Best known now as the railway stop for nearby Saint-Tropez, Saint-Raphaël had its heyday a century ago.

The town's centre is a palm-lined modern sea-front (the old one was destroyed during the Second World War) with an ornamental fountain and pyramid commemorating Napoleon's debarkation after the 1799 Egyptian victories.

In days gone by, there was a small holiday resort here for Romans based in Fréjus. It stood more or less on the site of the present casino — if you can imagine the clicking roulette tables replaced by luxurious tile baths and fish ponds.

The 12th-century Templars' church in the old town is surmounted with a massive watch-tower replacing the right-hand apse.

Fréjus

Little remains of the busy Roman market town of Fréjus (Forum Julii) founded in 49 B.C. The big harbour, built by Augustus into a great naval base and shipyard, has been completely filled up with silt deposits and replaced by modern Fréjus. A good part of the town was rebuilt after the 1959 catastrophe, when a dam upstream over the River Reyran broke, killing over 400 people.

Stopping point on the Esterel: splendid views at every turn.

Most impressive of the Roman vestiges is the **arena,** a restored grey-green construction which could seat 10,000 spectators—nearly as large as the arenas of Arles and Nîmes. It's closed on Tuesdays. During the season, bullfights are held here. Other Roman ruins include a theatre and big reddish arches of the aqueduct that brought water in from the River Siagnole.

Nearly razed by Saracens in the 10th century, Fréjus was revived in 990 by Bishop Riculphe, who established a fortified **episcopal city** here with a cathedral, baptistery, cloister and bishop's palace.

After entering the carved Renaissance doors (ask for the protecting panels to be opened), you see the **baptistery** on the left through an iron grille. One of the oldest religious buildings in France (late 4th to early

Provincial Colosseum—Roman arena at Fréjus held 10,000 people.

5th century), the octagonal baptistery is punctuated by handsome black granite columns with Corinthian capitals (from the ancient Fréjus forum). The terra-cotta baptismal bowl, the original, was unearthed in the course of archaeological research.

Ring a bell on the iron gate to visit the **cloister**—with its double-deckered arcade and garden with a well, roses and cypress trees. The ceiling of the upstairs arcade is decorated with some amusing 14th-century creatures—imaginative scenes from the Apocalypse. An archaeological museum adjoining the cloister has Gallo-Roman remains.

The 10th-12th-century **cathedral,** with its "broken cradle" vaulting, exemplifies the early Gothic style of the region. It was built on the site of a Roman temple dedicated to Jupiter.

Côte des Maures

On the way to Saint-Tropez, you'll pass through the attractive little town of SAINTE-MAXIME, with a casino, a minute beach and a wide promenade. In the summer it's packed with people who would love to be in Saint-Tropez but can't find a hotel room there.

Saint-Tropez

It barely manages to with its glamorous r celebrity escapades, of its little port, cafés filled with fashionable people, chic boutiques and casual nudity on nearby beaches.

Brigitte Bardot avoids the crowds now, but other stars still come out at night to haunt the "in" cafés and discotheques. In Saint-Tropez more than any other place on the Riviera you feel an unspoken desire to wear the right tee-shirt, be seen with the right people, show up in certain places at certain times of day or night. The atmosphere is enlivened by clusters of motorcycles roaring by, as well as haughty mannequins and golden boys with big dogs. In winter it reverts back to an easy-going fishing town.

Saint-Tropez weathers its own snobbery while cultivating its legends. The name comes from a Roman Christian, Torpes (an officer of the capricious Nero), who was martyred in Pisa in A.D. 68. The headless body, put adrift in a small boat with a dog and a cock, came ashore in the Var region. In the local church you can see a tableau of the body drifting along with its animal companion, as well as a wide-eyed **63** sculpture of the saint himself, neatly mustachioed, surrounded with a lacy halo, his chest covered with heart-shaped medals.

The town was battered several times by the Saracens, and recently by the German occupation and invasions of World War II. But the gallant little fishing village always managed to come back; in 1637 it routed a fleet of invading Spanish ships and still celebrates the victory in May with the Bravade, a fête that also honours St. Tropez himself. The natives get out their muskets, don 17th and 18th-century costumes and happily fire blanks all over the place in noisy parades with fife, drums, fireworks and cannon shots from the old fort. (There is a similar but less important festival in mid-June.)

First "discovered" by the French writer Guy de Maupassant, Saint-Tropez became very fashionable in the twenties,

Market day—gossip and good humour are order of the day.

when it was visited and painted by Dunoyer de Segonzac, Bonnard, Dufy and Signac; Colette wrote reams in her villa here, La Treille Muscate.

After World War II, the town managed to put itself together again in its former style, wisely rejecting plans for modern urban development.

You can't miss the **port** with its restless crowds, shiny yachts and pastel houses with red tile roofs, most of them rebuilt in the old fishermen's style. Nearby the plane-tree-shaded **Place des Lices** is crowded with local colour: a food market takes over several mornings a week, and *pétanque* (bowls) games are the centre of interest in late afternoon.

The **Musée de l'Annonciade,** a former chapel situated on the west side of the port, houses an **65** excellent collection of Impressionist and Post-Impressionist works. Many of the artists lived in and loved Saint-Tropez. You can view paintings by Signac, Van Dongen, Dufy, Bonnard and others in rooms lit by refracted Saint-Tropez sunshine. Outside, the quay space is crowded with contemporary artists, trying their best to sell their work, which can only be called "wares" compared to the contents of the Annonciade.

A short walk behind the Quai Jean-Jaurès will take you to the old town — through an arcade by La Ponche (the old fishing port), past narrow old buildings now housing expensive hotels and boutiques, to the 17th-century **Citadel** on top of the hill.

The moat, surrounded with

Saint-Tropez: sun and games at Tahiti beach; a junior gourmet.

greenery, is living quarters for preening peacocks, a few duck and deer. The Musée de la Marine here contains souvenirs of a locally born hero, Admiral de Suffren (who took his fleet on an odyssey around the Cape of Good Hope in 1781), model ships and diving equipment.

Saint-Tropez is noted for its beaches. Nearby ones like the Plage des Graniers and the Bouillabaisse are popular with local people on weekends, but holiday visitors look down their noses at them. They drive out to Les Salins or the vast sandy crescent (6 miles long) that stretches in front of green vineyards from Tahiti beach via Pampelonne to Cap Camarat.

Smooth-sanded and bordering a clear aquamarine sea, the beaches are fully equipped in summer with all manner of huts and shacks to furnish mattresses, umbrellas and sustenance to sunbathers. Part of the beach is traditionally given over to nudists — of all shapes; other areas are more or less discreet and more or less chic; each has its own style. Every summer the beautiful people gravitate to the bar-restaurant-beach of the moment.

More Ports and Hill Towns

Saint-Tropez is surrounded by delightful spots to visit when

you've had enough of the beach scene. A short trip will take you to GASSIN and RAMATUELLE— towns with panoramic views and pleasant restaurants— and the ruins of MOULINS DE PAILLAS. They provide an introduction to the **Maures** mountains, the oldest geological mass of Provence: worn-down cristalline hills, green and covered with pines and scrub trees.

Going north into the Maures over a long road full of hairpin bends, through thick forests of chestnut and cork, you come to LA GARDE-FREINET. At 1,329 feet, the town is considerably cooler than the coast. It has a natural, unspoilt charm that attracts crowd-weary Parisians. It also makes a living off the land—corks and chestnuts.

The ruins of an old fortress evoke the last stand of the marauding Saracens. For several centuries these pirates of Arab origin managed to hold out here as they pillaged the towns below—until they were thrown out in 973.

If you're pressed for time, forget La Garde-Freinet but stop at GRIMAUD—best in the late afternoon, when you can look out to the sea through the Provençal lotus trees and enjoy a drink in a local café. Grimaud was once the fiefdom of Gibalin (Ghibellin) de Grimaldi.

The fortress ruins stand up in piles of stony remnants against a grassy hill. A sign warns you not to poke around here because of the danger of falling rocks, but you can take a look at the simple, barrel-vaulted 11th-century Templars' church (restored version) and arcaded charterhouse.

Inland, the place to find an old
68 *fortress and fragrant fresh herbs.*

PORT-GRIMAUD, 6.5 kilometres downhill on the bay of Saint-Tropez, is the French modern version of Venice. Designed by François Spoerry and opened in 1964, it is a series of artificial canals built on marshland, lined with pleasant little houses and terraces painted in the same colours as Saint-Tropez.

For most French people, the Riviera stops at Saint-Tropez (some even say Saint-Raphaël), but the coast does go on. Not always the prettiest stretch, it is spoiled in parts by 20th-century concrete construction.

Still reasonably pleasant, however, are a string of small resort towns — LA CROIX-VALMER, CAVALAIRE, RAYOL and PRAMOUSQUIER — in flowered settings under the Maures hills.

LE LAVANDOU, originally a colourful spot, has suffered from urbanism, though it's still quite popular. The town has a pretty beachside promenade and is a good starting-point for excursions. Uphill, you'll find BORMES-LES-MIMOSAS, a lovely retreat that lives up to its name—blooming not only with mimosa, but oleander, roses, geraniums and bougainvillea.

Hyères is the "granny" of Mediterranean resorts. The French were coming here in the 18th century, when the English

started to winter at Nice. On the tree-shaded Place de la République, you'll see a 13th-century **church** where St. Louis, King of France, prayed after his return from a crusade in 1254; Hyères was the landing port for returning crusaders, though they disembarked at what is now the middle of town. Today modern boulevards run right over the old harbour.

Hyères is a busy city featuring an uphill market street, Rue Massillon (go in the morning

Instead of taking a noon siesta, this fisherman repairs his nets.

when it's in full swing), the old town, an ancient Templars' building and the Eglise Saint-Paul (a Gothic church renovated in the 16th century). From the square you have a panoramic view.

Iles d'Hyères

Also known as the Iles d'Or ("golden islands") because of their shiny, mica-shot rocks—sometimes mistaken for gold—they are three: Levant, Port-Cros and Porquerolles. You can easily visit them by ferry from Hyères and Le Lavandou or even from Cavalaire or Toulon.

The rocky **Ile du Levant** is France's nudist capital. You can keep your trousers on, but refrain from obvious gawking and photography: the *naturistes* don't like to be treated as curiosities. The eastern half **71** of the island is seriously off-limits—a naval base.

Next to the Levant lies the smaller **Ile de Port-Cros,** covered with steep myrtle- and heather-decked hills and an abundance of bird life. This protected national park area boasts resident flamingoes, turtle-doves, cormorants and puffins, plus rare flowers, especially orchids, and mushrooms in season (boletus and chanterelles).

The largest island, **Porquerolles** (5 miles long, 2 miles wide), is another enchanting setting, with a series of beaches along the north side (where the boat lands) and steep cliffs on the south coast. There are some excellent small beaches and coves for bathing on these islands, but you'll probably not be alone in the high season.

From Toulon to Marseilles

Toulon
Pop. 186,000

Military buffs love Toulon, France's big naval port, which reeks of maritime history. Its picturesque seafront was devastated during World War II, but even now with its modern concrete seaport blocks, it retains a certain dignity.

Toulon was pushed into prominence in the 17th century by Cardinal Richelieu, who saw the potential of a great natural harbour. Under Louis XIV, the military engineer Vauban was commissioned to fortify and enlarge the facilities.

World War II was a tragedy for the naval centre. Nearly the whole French fleet was

MARSEILLES–TOULON

scuttled on November 27, 1942, to keep it from falling into German hands. Two years later the port was battered by Allied troops, and then the Germans blew up their installations before leaving, wreaking more havoc. But with modern reconstruction, Toulon has regained its former importance.

Broad, busy Boulevard de Strasbourg (off Place de la Liberté) runs through the heart of Toulon, slicing the city in half. On the north is the newer, more residential area; to the south, the remains of the **old town**. Head in this direction for Place Puget, a charming Provençal square (just behind the Municipal Theatre) with a dolphin fountain and lots of greenery. Downhill is the narrow market street, Rue d'Alger, a favourite for evening strolling.

Off to the left, the cathedral, **Sainte-Marie-Majeure,** has a handsome baroque façade and belfry (18th century). Another block east is the Cours Lafayette, one of the most animated indoor-outdoor market streets in Europe, where you can buy everything from flowers to leather souvenirs. History enthusiasts can visit the nearby Musée Historique du Vieux-Toulon.

The **port** is a particularly lively part of town. See the magnificently muscled caryatids that guard the entrance to the **Musée Naval.** They look as if they were shouldering the world—and they're about all that's left of the old port. The museum (closed Tuesdays) contains some impressive boat models.

Across from the public garden in the west central part of town is the **Musée d'Art et d'Archéologie** (closed Mondays and Thursdays). It possesses a very good collection of Oriental art (Tibet, India, Japan and especially China), plus paintings from several periods and countries.

Mont Faron (1,778 feet) commands a grandiose view of Toulon, the surrounding mountains and the coast. You can get there by car via a steep, sinuous route or take a *téléphérique* from the Faron Corniche. Close to the peak is the Tour Beaumont, a fairly new war museum containing a wealth of information about the Liberation.

Inland excursions from Toulon include **Le Gros Cerveau** mountain with its magnificent panorama, the rugged **Gorges d'Ollioules,** the 16th-century castle remnants of **Evenos** and another look-out point at **Mont Caume.** If you have time to **73** venture further north, the **Massif de la Sainte-Baume** offers the irregular hilly landscape typical of Provence, a venerable forest and a stunning view from **Saint-Pilon.**

Côte des Calanques

The limestone coastline between Toulon and Marseilles is riddled with deep, uneven inlets *(calanques)*. This stretch, backed by the green scrub growth of the *maquis*, has in-evitably spawned holiday developments. But you can still find attractive natural sites.

Well-sheltered SANARY, with sandy beaches and an old port, is the first town you come to on the Baies du Soleil (sunny bays). **Bandol** takes honours as the area's leading resort. It has a mild climate and long beach lined with housing developments. It is known for its vineyards which produce good red and white wine.

You can make a pleasant

side trip to the privately owned island of **Bendor.** This recently developed site boasts a reproduction of a Provençal village and museums devoted to the sea and to wine.

One of the world's largest shipyards, LA CIOTAT has managed to retain a small bit of its original charm. Against the background of towering cranes and steel hulls of the busy modern shipyard, the old fishing port holds out doggedly— typically Provençal with nets, small boats and colourful houses.

The port of **Cassis** may seem familiar — paintings of it by artists like Vlaminck, Matisse and Dufy hang in museums all over the world. Today you'll see the same gaily-coloured stucco houses and crisp little triangular sails bobbing on the clear blue water, with the rocks

Limestone cliffs of Calanques drop off abruptly into the sea.

of La Gardiole or the tree-covered Cap Canaille hovering in the background.

Cassis is mainly known for its incomparable shellfish, its *bouillabaisse* (fish soup) and its white wine, appreciated all over the south (but not to be confused with the *cassis,* blackcurrant, syrup or liqueur).

From Cassis you'll probably want to visit some *calanques,* best done in a rented boat or on a tour. The most spectacular of them all is **d'En Vau**—a mini-fjord with limpid blue-green water fingering through the rocky cliffs to a minute crescent of a white beach.

Marseilles

Though not really part of the French Riviera, this great city of one million (*Marseille* to the French) merits a visit for many reasons. France's largest port, its second largest metropolis and its oldest, Marseilles has always played a major role in the country's history.

If offers excellent shopping, an international atmosphere, big industry, interesting museums and very good food: some of the best *bouillabaisse* on the coast is to be found here, particularly around the famous Canebière area.

Be sure to wander around the old port, first used by the Phoceans in 600 B.C., and to see the impressive facilities of the modern port. You can also tour it by boat.

The Marseillaise

France's bellicose national anthem is not really a local creation. Written by an Alsatian, Rouget de Lisle, it was taken up by Marseilles revolutionaries marching to Paris in 1792. On their arrival, they caused a sensation, and the song was immediately named: *La Marseillaise.*

Maritime parking lot in Marseilles for small craft and fishing boats.

What to Do

Museums

The Riviera is studded with excellent museums (some described more fully under town headings). Schedules tend to be a bit chaotic: most museums are open mornings 9 or 10 to noon, and afternoons 2 to 6 (winter), 3 to 7 (summer).

Antibes

All the museums are closed Tuesdays and in November.
Musée Grimaldi-Picasso, Place du Château, prodigious collection of Picasso's works (see p. 44).

Musée Archéologique, Bastion Saint-André, antiquities from the region.

Musée Naval et Napoléonien, Eden-Roc Cap d'Antibes, Napoleonic souvenirs.

Beaulieu

Villa Kérylos, open afternoons only; closed Mondays, November (see p. 30).

Biot

Musée National Fernand Léger, impressive one-man retrospective; open every day (see p. 46).

Cagnes-sur-Mer
Château-Musée, modern art works and olive museum; closed Tuesdays and October 15 to November 15 (see p. 47).

Cannes
Musée de la Castre, Le Suquet, eclectic collection; closed Monday, public holidays and November (see p. 58).

Grasse
Musée d'Art et d'Histoire de Provence (Fragonard), closed Monday, 2nd and 3rd Sunday each month and November (see p. 53).

La Napoule
Château (Henry Clews Foundation), impressive sculptures in a stylish setting; open in the summer 5–6 p.m., in winter 3–5 p.m. (see p. 59).

Monaco
Most interesting are the rooms of the *Palais du Prince* (open July and August only), the *Musée Océanographique* and the *Musée National* (see pp. 40–42).

Nice
Musée Masséna, 35, Promenade des Anglais, an old mansion with a good collection of Empire furnishings, historical exhibits, paintings from the 15th-16th-century Nice school, Impressionist paintings; closed Monday, public holidays.

Musée des Beaux-Arts Jules-Chéret, 33, avenue des Baumettes, outstanding Impressionist paintings and lovely pastels by Chéret, works by painter Gustav-Adolf Mossa, a symbolist whose eerie, intricate dream-fantasies deserve to be better known; closed Monday, public holidays.

Palais Lascaris, baroque palace in the heart of old Nice (see p. 22–23).

Musée du Vieux-Logis, 59, avenue Saint-Barthélemy, historical collection featuring Gothic statuary, religious paintings and stained glass; open Wednesday, Thursday, Saturday, 1st Sunday of every month, afternoons only.

Musée de Malacologie, 3, cours Saleya, seashells galore; closed Sunday and Monday.

Musée de Terra Amata, 25, boulevard Carnot, an engaging view of prehistoric man around Nice; closed Monday.

Musée Matisse et d'Archéologie, 164, avenue des Arènes, Cimiez; closed Monday (except in summer) and November (see p. 26–27).

Musée Chagall, avenue du Docteur-Ménard, Chagall's biblical themes in a modern setting; closed Tuesday.

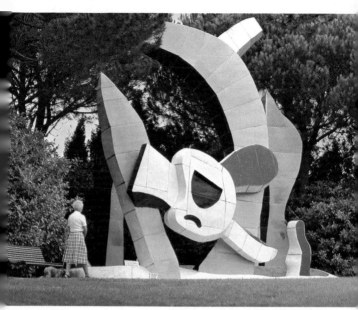

Monumental sculpture by Léger stands near his museum in Biot.

Saint-Jean-Cap-Ferrat
Fondation Ephrussi de Rothschild, "Belle Epoque" dwelling and gardens; closed Monday and November (see p. 30).

Saint-Paul-de-Vence
Fondation Maeght, one of the world's great modern art museums; open every day (see p. 49).

Saint-Tropez
Musée de l'Annonciade, a sunny display of 20th-century paintings on the old port; closed Tuesday, November (see p. 65).

Vence
La Chapelle du Rosaire, the famous Matisse chapel; open May–September 4–5 p.m., October–May on Tuesdays and Thursdays 10–11.30 a.m. **79**

For Children

Besides the myriad of sporting activities, there's lots to amuse children around the Riviera. Monaco, Cap Ferrat (don't miss the afternoon monkey show here), Fréjus and Toulon all have zoos.

The Monaco Oceanographic Museum has an excellent aquarium, while Marineland between Antibes and Biot offers penguins, seals and an afternoon dolphin show.

Monaco's Musée National features beautifully dressed dolls and mechanical puppets that perform wind-up tricks. The Monaco wax museum is also a favourite with children.

Brilliant bouquet crowns every important festival on the Riviera.

Festivals and Other Events

The Riviera's calendar is filled with festivals and religious pageants (especially around Lent, Easter and Christmas), plus major artistic and sporting events. Here are just a few of the outstanding ones:

January

Monte Carlo. Automobile Rally: the final leg of the 4,500-kilometre race roars through the city.

Cannes. MIDEM, international recording and music-publishing fair.

February

Nice. The Carnival fills the streets with floats, girls and gaiety in the two weeks preceding Shrove Tuesday.

Cannes. The mimosa festival celebrates nature.

Menton. During the Lemon Festival the town takes on a golden glow with citrus mosaics everywhere and parades.

March-April

Vence. Battle of Flowers, Provençal dancing (Easter).

May

Cannes. The International Film Festival stirs frenzy for a few weeks.

Saint-Tropez. The Bravade (see p. 64), is a costumed, noisy event commemorating local victories, May 16-18.

Monaco. The Grand Prix motor race.

Grasse. Rose Festival.

June

Antibes. Festival of St. Peter, sailors' religious celebration (last Sunday in June).

Nice. Festival of Sacred Music.

Saint-Tropez. Second Bravade (June 15).

July

Monaco. Concerts by the Orchestre National in the palace courtyard.

August

Menton. International Chamber Music Festival.

Roquebrune. Passion procession through streets of old town (August 5).

October

Cannes. VIDCOM, international video fair.

Shopping

Most shops and department stores are open from 8 or 9 a.m. to noon and from 2 to 7 p.m., Tuesday to Saturday (many stores close Monday). But hours can be casual. In the summer, small shops often close for longer periods in the middle of the day, but stay open later in the evening for the tourist trade. They may also open on Sundays.

Best Buys

The coast is a mouth-watering bazaar. You can find the best of everything French—jewellery, couturier clothing, silverware, crystal and even furs. In Nice (Rue de France), Cannes (Rue d'Antibes) and Monte Carlo (around the casino), the shopping areas are on a par with Paris.

In the mini-luxury category, good buys include silk scarves, perfumes, liqueurs and scented soaps. Sportswear is highly recommended, especially for women. The latest thing is always displayed in little boutiques and aggressively brushes your nose on the quayside at Saint-Tropez, where you can hardly go through the yards of tee-shirts without purchasing something.

Arts and Crafts

You'll see some beautiful pottery, glazed stoneware and ceramic work, particularly around Vallauris, Saint-Paul-de-Vence and Biot. Anything from simple ashtrays to entire dinner sets—plain, flowery, contemporary abstract, even some original Picasso designs.

The heavy, bubbled Biot glasswork in subtle colours fits well in a country-home setting.

Semi-precious stones, often set in jewellery, are abundant in shop windows. You'll

What to buy? Wooden antiques or an abstract print made yesterday.

frequently see olive-wood tables, stools, salad sets and bracelets—especially in the little towns behind Cannes.

The famous, attractively flowered Provençal cotton is ubiquitous; you can purchase it in bolts or made up into cushions, carryall bags, small shoulder bags, skirts or quilts.

Antiques and Art

You'll find old Provençal tables and commodes, brass clocks and candlesticks, copper cooking utensils, rare and common china patterns and plenty of "kitsch". Alas, most of the real bargains have already been snatched up.

If you're looking for art works, you'll find endless possibilities at all prices. There are hundreds of galleries selling paintings and sculptures by famous and local names: around the ports, painters turn out their rendition of the scene and sell at whatever price they can get.

Olives galore on market day in Place des Lices, Saint-Tropez.

Souvenirs

There's no lack in this area. Looking for a picture of the port of Cannes on a fringed satin flag, an ash-tray with the local château on it? Almost anything decorated with portraits of the royal family of Monaco? Your wishes will be easily gratified.

For philatelists, there are the beautifully printed Monaco stamps; for children, old favourites like sea-shell jewellery and traditionally costumed dolls.

Shopping Tips
If you have the time, compare prices in different shops before buying. You can always try to bargain at stands or small shops, but it rarely works, especially when a price tag is attached. Sometimes, though, you'll receive a special discount with a big purchase.

If you're returning home to a non-Common Market country, ask about the possibility of a refund of the value-added tax (TVA) in large stores. Usually only for purchases of at least 400 francs, this could mean 15 to 20 per cent off the bill. You must fill out a form, give a copy to the customs when leaving France and later receive your refund at home.

Shops with "duty-free" signs in the windows often give the TVA refund even on small purchases. The international airport is a good place to purchase duty-free items, especially liquor and perfumes.

Sports and Games

The Riviera's climate makes it ideal for outdoor sports, and facilities are generally first-rate.

Swimming
In the new official classification of beaches by cleanliness, the Côte d'Azur does well; of its 143 beaches, only 6 are "C"-grade (usable), all the others being "A"- or "B"-grade (impeccable or virtually pollution-free).

Beach concessionaires charge entry and/or changing-room fees at many bathing areas. You can also indulge yourself a little and rent a mattress (practically indispensable on some of the stony beaches). But of course, there are also free—if not always spic and span—public beaches. The other trick is a fee for parking. If you prefer a pool, there are many of them charging a small fee for entry.

Windsurfing
Windsurfing, or sailboarding, is one of the coast's fastest-growing sports. It is also one of the most difficult. Courses are given, and boards (*planche à voile*) can be hired in all the major resorts.

Water-skiing

Ski nautique exists at all the larger beaches (Nice, Cannes, Antibes and so on). Real daredevils go for kite-skiing.

Scuba Diving, Snorkelling

There are diving centres at Antibes, Cagnes, Cannes, Monte Carlo and Nice. Equipment may be hired and instruction arranged at centres in these localities.

Fishing

The piscine population of the Mediterranean is suffering from over-fishing and pollution. But you can spend a few pleasant hours with baited hook around the coast or take a day-tour on a fishing boat. Real sportsmen like to angle for trout in the mountain streams. Inquire about licence regulations.

Boating and Sailing

The coast is lined with first-class yacht facilities. If you require the best of everything but haven't brought your own boat, you can hire a 30-metre vessel with a ten-man crew and enjoy the "the life of Riley." Smaller boats, of course, are

The exuberance of scuba divers contrasts with the quiet joys of angling in a mountain stream.

also available for those with more modest requirements and tighter budgets. For an idea of what it might cost, see p. 103. Cannes and Antibes are the biggest rental centres.

Tennis

You find tennis courts almost everywhere along the coast. The proper attire and payment of an hourly court fee will admit you to most clubs. In summer you may have to book a day ahead.

Golf

The best in France—with scenic 18-hole courses at Biot, Mandelieu-La Napoule, Mougins, Valbonne (all clustered around Cannes), Monte Carlo (Mont-Agel), and a few 9-hole courses. You can hire clubs, though it's advisable to bring your own shoes and golf balls, as these are expensive in France.

Anyone can take a crack at it.

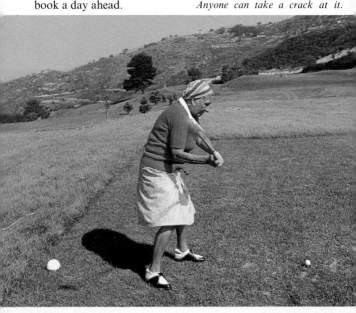

Horse-riding

There are lots of possibilities for riding, often "ranch" style in the country behind the coast.

Skiing

About two hours from the coast are 11 winter sports areas, some very well developed. Best-known are Isola 2000 (they teach the new graduated short-ski method there), Auron and Valberg.

Other Activities

You can play the local *pétanque* (or *boules*) if the natives will initiate you to this bowling game; but every sport is available somewhere—from regular bowling, judo and archery to table tennis. If you're feeling fit, hire a bicycle and pedal around the hills alongside the fanatics practising for semi- or professional races. The Riviera's modern racecourse is at Cros-de-Cagnes, near the Nice airport.

Nightlife

The Riviera is a night-crawler's dream. From the very first seaside aperitif to well after midnight or even till dawn, nocturnal activity is hectic. Some people can hardly drag themselves to the beach the next day. Possibilities range from "pub" crawling around some of the dock areas (Nice, Toulon) to the most elegant balls in the world, particularly at Monte Carlo.

Cultural Activities

On the dignified side, the coast offers the best in music and ballet. Monte Carlo's opera house features brilliant opera, concerts, ballet and theatre the year round; summer concerts in the palace courtyard are particularly popular (try to book in advance). Ticket prices for concerts and opera vary considerably.

Menton has a famous music festival in August; Nice, its own opera house with good theatre in the winter; Toulon, a municipal theatre that also presents concerts and ballet. The latest films are shown in French or dubbed in French.

Nightclubs and Discotheques

For slick floorshows or elegant dining and dancing, go to Nice, Monte Carlo or Cannes. As you would expect, the discotheque scene is frenetic but you can get in almost anywhere. (For an idea of nightclub and discotheque prices, see p. 103.) Monte Carlo has the

Well-heeled visitors enjoy sumptuous show at Monte Carlo casino.

most elegant discos, Saint-Tropez the prettiest clientele, and in between you'll find everything, with a particularly rowdy ambiance at Juan-les-Pins in summer. Dine late, because discos don't start to warm up till 11 p.m. or so.

Casinos

The tense atmosphere may not be apparent in the streets, but for some here gambling is a way of life. Monte Carlo started the ball rolling in 1860, and the other towns joined the profitable bandwagon 50 years later. Now at least 20 casinos operate between Menton and Sainte-Maxime.

You'll find every game going —from the non-stop slot machines to baccarat. The casinos usually open sometime after 3 p.m. (hours vary) and stay open till the last discouraged customer quits, but for early birds, Monte Carlo's main casino opens at 10 a.m.

Entry prices vary from place to place, but all the casinos charge a minimum fee that is valid for a week. Most establishments ask to see your passport.

Wining and Dining

Wandering through the streets of a southern French town, you can often guess what's cooking for dinner. Marvellous aromas — of fresh rosemary or thyme, all-pervading garlic, fragrant olive oil, the smoky smell of charcoal-broiled meat or fish — waft through the air. Add to that images of the plump and juicy tomatoes, glistening green and red peppers, dark purple aubergines, silvery sardines, all fresh from the market-place, and you'll be ready to sit down to eat.

French cooking reaches great peaks in Provence*. Some of the country's best restaurants here offer exquisite (and expensive) food in incomparable settings. But food can also be deliciously simple with robust flavours. When you see *à la provençale* on a menu, you can be fairly sure garlic, tomato and herbs are part of the recipe. And don't shy away from garlic and onions: they're eminently appropriate in this climate.

---

*For a comprehensive glossary of French culinary terms and how to order wine, ask your bookshop for the Berlitz EUROPEAN MENU READER.

Soup and Salad

Pistou is practically a whole meal — a thick vegetable soup made with beans, onions or leeks, fresh herbs, especially basil, and usually garlic, topped with freshly grated cheese.

Soupe de poisson can also fill you up for hours. Made with available fish leftovers, tomato, saffron, garlic and onions, it's served with generous garnishings of toast rounds, grated cheese and *rouille*, a hot tomato-garlic-flavoured mayonnaise. *Bourride* is thicker and richer, with lots of fish ground up in it.

Speaking of garlic, try a bracing *aïoli* (when you don't have any important social engagements). You dip boiled fish, potatoes, green beans and so on in the heavily perfumed mayonnaise.

The renowned *salade niçoise* can be a treat. Essential ingredients include tomato, anchovies, radishes, green peppers, olives, sometimes cucumbers and artichoke hearts, well doused in a vinaigrette dressing. Tuna, celery, green beans, hard-boiled egg quarters and a few lettuce leaves (the latter anathema to the purists) may complete the picture.

Endless mixed salads are offered, many with ham and cheese or seafood. *Salade anti-*

Bouillabaisse

It's only fish stew, but the mystique surrounding it is substantial enough to fill a Proustian novel. Every chef has his own idea: some say it's heresy to include spiny lobster and that mussels are only for Parisians. Marseilles chefs are appalled by their Toulon confreres' addition of potatoes.

The important thing is really the fresh local seafood — with fascinating names like *rascasse*, *baudroie*, *chapon* and *Saint-Pierre*. These can be translated but mean next to nothing away from the Mediterranean. The fish are served in their own broth highly flavoured with wine, cayenne and saffron, and accompanied by crunchy croutons and garlicky red-hot *rouille*.

boise usually combines cooked diced fish and anchovy fillets with green peppers, beetroot, rice and capers with vinaigrette dressing. *Crudités*, a raw vegetable salad, makes a nice light first course.

Fish

On the Riviera, the aristocrat of fish is the *loup de mer* (sea bass), best prepared with fennel, flamed. *Daurade*, a tender white fish (gilt-head or sea bream), costs less; it's usually grilled or baked with onion, tomato and lemon juice and a dash of wine, occasionally with garlic and a *pastis* (anis) flavouring. *Rouget* (red mullet) may be served grilled or *en papillotte* (baked in foil with lemon wedges).

The grilled *scampi* (prawns) you'll see on menus everywhere can be good, but they're invariably imported and frozen. *Langouste*, or spiny lobster, costs a king's ransom. It's eaten cold with mayonnaise or hot in a tomato-and-cognac-flavoured sauce *(à l'américaine)*.

Mussels *(moules)* are popular *à la marinière* (in white wine), in soup or with savoury stuffings. A lowly but tempting gourmandise is *friture de mer*, crisp-fried small fish to be eaten like chips.

Meat and Poultry

Steak turns up in various fashions, but the good cuts *(entrecôte, côte de bœuf, faux-filet, filet)* are as tasty charcoal-broiled with fresh herbs as with sauces. *Saignant* means rare; *bleu*, almost raw; *à point*, medium done.

Mougins—one of the places to find the best in French cuisine.

Lamb is succulent in the spring; you'll most often see *gigot d'agneau* or *côtes d'agneau grillées aux herbes* (leg of lamb or grilled chops with herbs), which the French serve medium rare. *Brochettes*, or skewered kebabs, can be delicious, though the quality depends on the meat chosen by the chef.

Daube de bœuf is a traditional beef stew particularly good in Nice. With its aromatic brown, wine-flavoured mushroom sauce, accompanied by freshly made noodles *(pâtes fraîches)*, it can be memorable. *Estouffade*, a variation on the theme, adds black olives to the sauce.

Veal is often of Italian inspiration, as in breaded-fried *esca-*

Relaxed aperitif hour in Menton on the lively Place aux Herbes.

lopes milanaises (scaloppini). But *alouettes sans têtes* are not "headless larks" as the translation would imply: they're small rolled veal cutlets with stuffing (veal birds).

Even tripe-haters are converted by the Niçois version of this dish *(tripes niçoises)*: a superb concoction simmered in olive oil, white wine, tomato, onion, garlic and herbs.

Pieds et paquets, a Marseilles speciality, consists of stuffed tripe and sheeps' trotters cooked with bacon, onion, carrot rounds, white wine, garlic and sometimes tomato.

Chickens are frequently spit-roasted with herbs *(poulet rôti aux herbes)*; *poulet niçoise* is a local fricassee made with white wine, stock, herbs, tomatoes and black olives. Rabbit *(lapin)* can be quite tender, like chicken, and might be served in a mustard sauce or *à la provençale*.

In season (autumn/winter), the menu may list partridge *(perdreau)*, pigeon or quail *(caille)* often served with a grape sauce *(aux raisins)*, or boar *(marcassin* or *sanglier)*.

Pasta and Vegetables

The Italian influence is strong around Menton and Nice, becoming less so as you go west. You'll often find superb pasta —ravioli, cannelloni, fettuccine, lasagne—rivalling Italy's best.

But the glory of southern France is its fresh vegetables. *Ratatouille* — the celebrated vegetable stew made with tomatoes, onions, aubergine (eggplant), marrow (zucchini) and green peppers—practically stands as a meal in itself, either hot or cold. You'll also find delicious stuffed aubergines, marrow and tomatoes well seasoned with local herbs.

Asparagus *(asperges)* are superb warm with melted butter or hollandaise sauce or cold with *vinaigrette*. Artichokes receive the same treatment or may appear with meat or herb stuffings.

Cheese and Dessert

In the south you can usually eat classics from the 300-odd varieties of French cheese. But don't miss out on the regionally made goat or sheeps'-milk cheeses *(fromages de chèvre, de brebis)*. A few good names: *tomme de Sospel, tomme de chèvre de montagne, brousse de la Vésubie, cabécou, poivre d'âne*.

For dessert, nothing can rival the local fruits in season. Savour the fat, dark-red strawberries (April to July) dipped in *crème fraîche* (a slightly acid **95** double cream). Melons of all kinds (from Cavaillon, near Aix, they're renowned) taste sweeter than usual. Figs and peaches are equally good. Ices are refreshing, especially the fruit *sorbets.* You can satisfy a sweet tooth with all kinds of fruit tarts and local pastries: *ganses* (small fried cakes topped with sugar), *pignons* (buttery *croissants* with pine-nuts) and the famed *tarte tropézienne* of Saint-Tropez—a rich yellow cake with custard filling and coarse-sugar topping.

Quick Snacks

Cafés serve hearty sandwiches on long chunks of French bread (pâté, ham or cheese). Thin-sliced sandwich bread *(pain de mie)* is used for the delicious *croque-monsieur* (toasted ham-and-cheese sandwich). Omelettes are always reliable fare.

Tian is a local term vaguely covering warm or cold stuffed pastry or omelettes sold by street vendors and in some restaurants. The filling is usually an egg-custard, green vegetable mixture. *Tourtes* are pastry turnovers with similar vegetable stuffings.

Another popular local item (great at the beach) is *pan bagnat*—essentially a huge round sandwich filled with tomatoes, hard-boiled egg, olives, anchovies, and sliced onions, moistened with olive oil.

Also noteworthy are the excellent thin-crusted pizzas (all flavours) and *pissaladière:* a savoury tart with a topping of onion, anchovies, black olives and sometimes tomatoes.

Aperitifs and Wine

You can find the world's most sophisticated cocktails in the big hotel bars down here. If you order a martini, specify *un dry* or you might get Martini, the sweet Italian vermouth. Every little bar-café sells scotch, various imported and domestic beers, many non-alcoholic drinks. A very refreshing drink is *citron pressé* (fresh-squeezed lemon juice).

The number one local drink, of course, is *pastis.* This anise-flavoured yellow liquid turns milky when you add water—very refreshing on a warm day.

Vintage wines from all over France are available in the better restaurants, but for daily fare stick to the local product—white, red and especially rosé.

The best regional wines bear an *appellation contrôlée* (A.C.) label, guaranteeing place of origin and government-controlled quality. Four areas are given these labels: La Palette, Cassis, Bandol and Bellet.

La Palette (grown at Meyreuil, near Aix) comes from country thick with pines or herbs whose fragrances are said to permeate the wines. They exist in red and white (most notable — *Château Simone*). Cassis produces a fine red wine, but the flowery-light white wine is a special treat, particularly with shellfish.

Near Toulon, Bandol wine grows in a particularly favoured setting, producing some whites and lots of fruity rosés and reds, the latter particularly good; look for *Domaine des Tempiers*. Bellet is the fourth A.C. area, on precariously sloped vineyards above Nice, producing white, red and rosé wines.

Further down the official scale, wines marked V.D.Q.S. *(vin délimité de qualité supérieure)* appear all over the south.

Mid-morning snack in old Nice: socca, an outsized fried pancake.

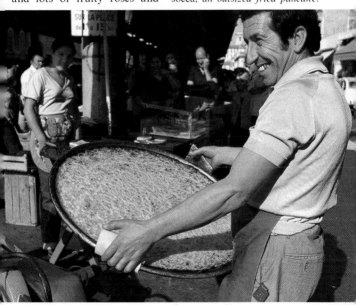

Wine Guidelines

The fresh, slightly fruity qualities of Provençal white wine make it the perfect accompaniment to fish and shellfish. Sometimes the wines lack acidity because of the constant sunshine.

Rosé is much-maligned by wine snobs, who treat it as a poor compromise between white and red. But in Provence, it's another matter; even connoisseurs enjoy a well-chilled bottle with meals (particularly chicken or fish dishes) or as an aperitif. Rosés with the V.D.Q.S. label are reliably good; Tavel and Lirac, grown near Avignon, are famous.

The colour of rosé is important: it should be light to rosy *pink*, not orange, which shows it has oxidized prematurely.

Red wines are gaining in both virtue and renown in the south. The A.C. areas now produce honourable reds, some to be drunk quite young and fresh (preferably cool), others age gracefully. *Château Vignelaure*, grown northeast of Aix, is a special case.

Don't be surprised by the lack of vintage year on the labels of wine from Provence. Most are meant to be served very young (often within the year) and don't benefit from ageing.

To Help You Order...

Do you have a table?
Do you have a set-price menu?

Avez-vous une table?
Avez-vous un menu à prix fixe?

I'd like a/an/some...

J'aimerais…

beer	une bière	menu	la carte
butter	du beurre	milk	du lait
bread	du pain	mineral water	de l'eau minérale
coffee	un café		
dessert	un dessert	potatoes	des pommes de terre
egg	un œuf		
fish	du poisson	salad	une salade
fruit	un fruit	sandwich	un sandwich
glass	un verre	soup	de la soupe
ice-cream	une glace	sugar	du sucre
lemon	du citron	tea	du thé
meat	de la viande	wine	du vin

... and Read the Menu

agneau	lamb	langouste	spiny lobster
ail	garlic	langoustine	prawn
anchois	anchovy	langue	tongue
artichaut	artichoke	lapin	rabbit
asperges	asparagus	lièvre	hare
aubergine	eggplant	loup de mer	sea-bass
bifteck	steak	macédoine	fruit salad
bœuf	beef	de fruits	
caille	quail	médaillon	tenderloin
calmar	squid	moules	mussels
canard, caneton	duck	moutarde	mustard
cervelle	brains	mulet	grey mullet
chèvre, cabri	goat	navets	turnips
chou	cabbage	nouilles	noodles
chou-fleur	cauliflower	oignons	onions
choux de	brussels sprouts	oseille	sorrel
Bruxelles		petits pois	peas
concombre	cucumber	pintade	guinea fowl
côte, côtelette	chop, cutlet	poisson	fish
courgettes	baby marrow (zucchini)	poireaux	leeks
coquelet	baby chicken	pomme	apple
coquilles	scallops	porc	pork
Saint-Jacques		poulet	chicken
crevettes	shrimps	prunes	plums
daurade	gilt-head (fish)	radis	radishes
écrevisse	crayfish	raisins	grapes
endive	chicory (endive)	ris de veau	sweetbreads
épinards	spinach	riz	rice
fenouil	fennel	rognons	kidneys
fèves	broad beans	rouget	red mullet
flageolets	dried beans	St. Pierre	John Dory (fish)
foie	liver	saucisse/	sausage/dried
fraises	strawberries	saucisson	sausage
framboises	raspberries	sorbet	water-ice
fruits de mer	seafood		(sherbet)
gigot (d'agneau)	leg (of lamb)	thon	tunny (tuna)
glace	ice, ice-cream	truffes	truffles
haricots verts	string beans	veau	veal
jambon	ham	volaille	chicken

99

How to Get There

The ever-changing air fares and airline regulations are complicated even for seasoned travellers. A reliable travel agent will be able to suggest a plan best suited to your timetable and budget.

When planning your trip, consult the Blueprint section in this book (pages 104 to 125), especially for ENTRY AND CUSTOMS FORMALITIES and HOTELS AND ACCOMMODATION. If looked through in advance, this section can help you prepare for your visit to the French Riviera.

BY AIR

From North America

Scheduled Flights: There are through flights to Nice every day from New York and several times a week from other U.S. cities. Passengers departing from other parts of the United States or Canada can travel via almost any European gateway city. Passengers from Montreal have the possibility of being routed through Casablanca.

Excursion rates offering a considerable saving on regular fares are available to passengers who can either travel within several fixed minimum or maximum time limits, travel off-season, buy tickets well in advance of departure or travel without advance reservations. Ask about APEX (advance purchase excursion) and Super APEX fares.

Charter Flights and Package Tours: Paris–Riviera package deals are frequently offered by tour organizers. Check the newspapers for the latest possibilities. There are charter flights available directly to the Riviera, or to many convenient gateway cities in Europe.

From the United Kingdom

Scheduled Flights: There are frequent non-stop flights to Nice from London and some direct flights from Manchester. An economical way to travel on scheduled flights is to book an "instant fare" to Paris the day before you want to go and take a connecting flight to Nice. There is also an excursion fare available if you stay for at least six days and no more than one month.

Charter Flights and Package Tours: Most tour organizers use scheduled airlines, although some charter flights are available in the summer. Many kinds of package tours are offered, including room and meals. Most travel agents recommend cancellation insurance which prevents your losing money in case illness or accident forces you to cancel your holiday.

From Australia

Besides the usual direct economy flights to Paris with unrestricted stop-overs, or flights through other European gateway cities with connections to Nice, there are excursion flights and package deals from Sydney. Trips to Paris for a specified number of days or excursions from Sydney to Nice via the East are the lowest-priced possibilities at present.

BY RAIL

Dependable train services exist to Folkestone from all over Great Britain. Boat crossings connect with trains from Calais to Nice and other French Riviera stations (the Flandres-Riviera Express, for example) with sleepers and meals available.

Eurailpass: Non-Europeans may travel on a flat-rate unlimited mileage ticket, valid for first-class rail travel anywhere in western Europe outside Great Britain. You must purchase this pass before leaving home. **Eurail Youthpass** offers second-class travel to anyone under 26. **Inter-rail cards** permit 30 days of unlimited rail travel in participating European countries and Morocco to people under 26 and to women over 60 and men over 65. In the country of issue, fares are given a 50% discount.

BY ROAD

Car ferries: It is advisable to book your car passage well in advance. The main routes link Dover and Folkestone with Dunkirk, Calais and Boulogne, Newhaven with Dieppe, and Weymouth with Cherbourg. You can also travel from Southampton to Le Havre.

By hovercraft: You can cross the Channel from Ramsgate or Dover to Calais in about 35 minutes for about the same price as the ferry.

By rail: Cars and passengers can make the journey together on special trains from London to Paris or Boulogne to the Riviera, allowing you to sleep en route.

Motoring is easy on the secondary roads in France which, though longer than the *autoroutes,* offer good scenery and are toll-free.

When to Go

July and August are the peak summer months when the crowds are drawn to France's sunniest beaches. These are the months when the climate is at its best, though spring and fall offer many days of mild weather with fewer visitors.

You may want to plan your holiday around one of the many events on the Riviera, such as Cannes' annual film festival in May.

Following are some monthly average temperatures:

		J	F	M	A	M	J	J	A	S	O	N	D
Air temperature	C	9	9	11	13	17	20	23	22	20	17	12	9
	F	48	48	52	55	63	68	73	72	68	63	54	48
Sea temperature	C	13	13	13	15	17	21	24	25	23	20	17	14
	F	55	55	55	59	63	70	75	77	73	68	63	57

Planning Your Budget

The following are some prices in French francs (F). However, they must be regarded as approximate; inflation in France, as elsewhere, rises steadily.

Baby-sitters. 30–50 F per hour, 150–200 F per day.

Bicycle and moped rental. Bicycle 37 F per day, deposit 450 F, moped 85 F per day, deposit 1,800 F.

Camping.*** 100 F for two persons per day including car and services, 12–25 F per extra person.

Car hire. *Renault 5* 112.80 F per day, 1.33 F per km., 1,258 F per week with unlimited mileage. *Talbot Simca Horizon* 140.70 F per day, 1.86 F per km., 1,592 F per week with unlimited mileage. *Peugeot 505* 196.70 F per day, 2.36 F per km., 2,249 F per week with unlimited mileage. Add 33.33% tax.

Cigarettes. French 5.70 F per packet of 20, foreign 7.80 F, French cigars 15–20 F for 20.

Entertainment. Cinema 29 F, admission to discotheque 80 F and up, casino 180 F for weekly card, cabaret 200 F, opera 60–200 F.

Guides. 300 F for half day, 500 F per day (plus meal).

Hairdressers. *Man's* haircut 40–80 F. *Woman's* haircut 60 F and up, blow-dry/shampoo and set 60 F and up, manicure 50 F and up.

Hotels (double room with bath, summer season—not including 15% service and breakfast). **** L 500–1,500 F, **** 320–680 F, *** 250–490 F, ** 180–260 F, * 110–250 F. *Youth hostel:* 25–35 F.

Meals and drinks. Continental breakfast 12–30 F, lunch/dinner in fairly good establishment 120–200 F, coffee 8 F, cognac 20–25 F, whisky or cocktail 25–30 F, beer 9 F, glass of wine 5 F and up, bottle of wine 25 F and up.

Sports. Water-skiing (4-minute run) 80–85 F, windsurfing (1 hour) 80–85 F, scuba diving 55 F per dive including equipment, all-day fishing expedition with local fisherman 200 F per person, speed boat 9 Hp. 800 F per day plus deposit, tennis 15–30 F per hour, golf green fee 110–140 F (caddies 100 F, rental of clubs 60 F).

Taxis. Meter starts at 8.50 F, plus 2.20–6.60 F per km.

BLUEPRINT for a Perfect Trip

An A-Z Summary of Practical Information and Facts

Contents

A star (*) following an entry indicates that relevant prices are to be found on page 103.
Listed after most entries is the appropriate French translation usually in the singular, plus a number of phrases that may come in handy during your stay in France.

AIRPORT *(aéroport)*. The Nice-Côte d'Azur international airport **A** (7 km. from Nice) is used by 20 airlines serving over 40 foreign destinations. Facilities include a currency-exchange bank, restaurants, bars, post office and car-rental agency as well as souvenir and duty-free shops. An airline bus leaves every 30 minutes for Nice, and another to Cannes stops at Antibes and Juan-les-Pins. A helicopter service connects the airport with Monaco.

The Marseilles-Marignane airport has direct connections with French and major European cities, Corsica and North Africa.

Where's the bus for...?	**D'où part le bus pour...?**

BABY-SITTERS* *(baby-sitter, garde d'enfants)*. The larger towns and **B** cities have baby-sitter services that advertise in the local papers. The best system is to first ask your hotel to help you find a sitter. You may be able to engage a hotel maid to "look in"' from time to time.

Can you get me a baby-sitter for tonight?	**Pouvez-vous me trouver une garde d'enfants pour ce soir?**

BICYCLE and MOTORCYCLE RENTAL* *(location de bicyclettes/de motocyclettes)*. It's possible to hire bicycles, mopeds, called *vélomoteurs*, motorcycles and scooters in most towns of the French Riviera. Be prepared to lay out a deposit.

Minimum age to ride a moped is 14; for scooters from 50 to 125 cc., 16 years; over 125 cc. it's 18. Crash-helmets are obligatory. Enquire about rentals at your hotel or the local tourist office *(syndicat d'initiative)*.

CAMPING* *(camping)*. Camping is extremely popular and very well **C** organized in the South of France. There are over 300 officially recognized sites in the Alpes-Maritimes and the Var, most of them offering attractive locations and good facilities. These sites are classified from one to four stars depending on their amenities.

C

A *camping interdit* notice means the site is forbidden to campers, and the sign isn't a joke. You can always try to obtain an owner's permission to camp on private property in the region, but your chances are not very good.

Excellent booklets, such as *Camping—Côte d'Azur* (Menton to Cannes) can be obtained through the French Tourist Office in your country (see TOURIST INFORMATION OFFICES). For the Var region, write to Promo-Var, Conseil Général du Var, 1, bd Foch, 83300 Draguignan.

In the summer season, it's important to book in advance.

May we camp here, please?	**Pouvons-nous camper ici, s'il vous plaît?**

CAR HIRE* *(location de voitures).* All major car-hire firms in France handle French-made cars and occasionally foreign makes. Locally based firms generally charge less than the international companies but give little or no choice of where you can return the car.

To hire a car you must produce a valid driving licence (held for at least one year) and your passport. Some firms set a minimum age at 21, others 25. Holders of major credit cards are normally exempt from deposit payments, otherwise you must pay a substantial (refundable) deposit for a car. Third-party insurance is usually automatically included, and with an extra fee per day you can obtain full insurance coverage.

I'd like to hire a car tomorrow.	**Je voudrais louer une voiture demain.**
for one day/a week	**pour une journée/une semaine**
Please include full insurance.	**Avec assurance tous risques, s'il vous plaît.**

CIGARETTES, CIGARS, TOBACCO* *(cigarettes; cigares; tabac).* Tobacco is a state monopoly in France, and the best place to buy your cigarettes is at an official *débit de tabac* (licensed tobacconist's). There are plenty of these—cafés and bars—bearing the conspicuous double red cone.

French cigarettes include brands with dark or light tobacco, with or without filter. Dozens of foreign brands are also available at higher prices. Pipe tobacco comes in a variety of cuts, from sweet to strong.

A pack of.../A box of matches, please.	**Un paquet de.../Une boîte d'allumettes, s'il vous plaît.**
filter-tipped/without filter	**avec/sans filtre**
light/dark tobacco	**du tabac blond/brun**

CLOTHING *(habillement)*. From May to October you can usually count on mild to hot weather and light summer clothing is best. On the other hand, be sure to take a warm jacket or wrap for cool evenings, and you'll appreciate a raincoat in the low season, even in late spring. Light wool clothing and an overcoat are necessary in the winter.

Anything goes on the Riviera, but each town has its code. Complete nudity is tolerated on some beaches (notably around Saint-Tropez and on the Ile du Levant); topless sunbathing is permitted in most places.

At night, *tenue correcte* is required in casinos — that is, a jacket and tie for men, dresses or neat slacks for women. When visiting churches, respectable clothing should be worn, though women are no longer expected to cover their heads.

COMMUNICATIONS

Post Office *(poste)*. You can identify French post offices by a sign with a stylized blue bird and/or the words *Postes et Télécommunications* or P & T. In cities the main post office is open from 8 a.m. to 5 p.m., Monday to Friday, and 8 a.m. to noon on Saturdays. In smaller towns the hours are from 8.30 a.m. to noon, and 2.30 to 5 or 6 p.m., Monday to Friday; 8 a.m. to noon on Saturdays.

In addition to normal mail service, you can make local or long-distance telephone calls, send telegrams and receive or send money at any time at the post office.

Note: You can also buy stamps at a tobacconist's.

Mail *(courrier)*. If you don't know ahead of time where you're staying, you can have your mail addressed to *poste restante* (general delivery) in any town. Towns with more than one post office keep mail at the main post office. Take your passport with you for identification.

Telegrams *(télégramme)*. All local post offices accept telegrams, domestic or overseas. You may also dictate a telegram over the telephone (dial 001111).

Telephone *(téléphone)*. International or long-distance calls can be made from phone boxes, but if you need assistance in placing the call go to the post office or ask at your hotel. If you want to make a reverse-charge (collect) call, ask for *un appel en PCV* (pronounced: pay-say-vay). For a personal (person-to-person) call, specify *un appel avec préavis pour...* (naming the party you want to talk to).

Local calls can also be made from cafés, where you might have to buy a *jeton* (token) to put into the phone.

When calling long-distance in France, dial 16 and wait for the dialling tone, then dial the area code of the *département* followed by the number of the person you are calling.

To ring abroad from France, dial 19 followed, after the change of tone, by the country's number (listed in all boxes), the area code and the subscriber's number. If direct dialling is not available to that country or if you don't know the telephone number of the subscriber, dial 19 and wait for the tone, then dial 33 followed by the code number of the country in question to reach the operator (UK 44, U.S.A. and Canada 1). If you do not know the number of the country, call the international information, 19-33-33.

It's cheaper to make long-distance trunk calls after 8 p.m.

express (special delivery)	**exprès**
airmail	**par avion**
registered	**recommandé**
A stamp for this letter/ postcard, please	**Un timbre pour cette lettre/ carte postale, s'il vous plaît.**
I want to send a telegram to...	**J'aimerais envoyer un télégramme à...**
Have you any mail for...?	**Avez-vous du courrier pour...?**
Can you get me this number in...?	**Pouvez-vous me donner ce numéro à...?**

COMPLAINTS *(réclamation)*

Hotels and restaurants. Complaints should be referred to the owner or manager of the establishment in question. If you fail to obtain on-the-spot satisfaction for your complaint, you can refer the matter to the nearest police station *(commissariat de police)*. If they cannot help, apply to the regional administration offices *préfecture* or *sous-préfecture)*, asking for the *service du tourisme*.

Bad merchandise; car repairs. Complain at once to the proprietor or manager. In the event of gross abuse, register your complaint at the local *commissariat*. For complaints about cars or car repairs, members of automobile associations can consult the Touring Club de France.

I'd like to make a complaint.	**J'ai une réclamation à faire.**

CONSULATES *(consulat)*. Most consulates are open, Monday to Friday, from 9 or 10 a.m. to 4 or 5 p.m. with an hour or so off for lunch. Schedules may change with the season, so it's best to call in advance.

Australia: (embassy) 4, rue Jean Rey, 75015 Paris; tel. 575 62 00.

Canada: 24, avenue du Prado, Marseilles 6ᵉ; tel. 37 19 37.

Eire: 71, boulevard Poincaré, Juan-les-Pins; tel. 61 08 85.

United Kingdom: 24, avenue du Prado, Marseilles 6ᵉ; tel. 53 43 32.

U.S.A.: 9, rue Armeny, Marseilles 6ᵉ; tel. 33 78 33;
36, rue Maréchal Joffre, 06000 Nice; tél. 88 89 55.

CONVERTER CHARTS. For fluid and distance measures, see pages 111-112. France uses the metric system.

Temperature

Length

Weight

COURTESIES. See also MEETING PEOPLE. The sunny climate of southern France makes for a good-natured but impetuous temperament. Though you'll hear lots of shouting, it's usually high-spirited discussion rather than real argument, and the shopkeepers and restaurant personnel are far more relaxed than in Paris.

In restaurants and cafés, *garçon* is the customary way to call a waiter (*mademoiselle* for a waitress), or you can simply say *s'il vous plaît*. The *maître d'hôtel* (headwaiter) and *sommelier* (wine steward) are addressed as *monsieur*.

French people kiss or shake hands when greeting each other or saying goodbye. When you're introduced to someone or meeting a friend you're expected to shake hands at least. Close friends are kissed on both cheeks.

C   If you stop a policeman or passerby to ask for directions, start with *excusez-moi, Monsieur/Madame*. Use your French, no matter how faulty, unless the person you're speaking to seems impatient and speaks your language well. Your effort will be appreciated.

Good day!	**Bonjour!**
I'm glad to meet you.	**Enchanté.**
How are you?	**Comment allez-vous?**

CRIME and THEFT *(délit; vol)*. If you have items of real value, keep them in the hotel safe and obtain a receipt for them; it's a good idea to leave large amounts of money and even your passport there as well.

Another wise precaution is to keep any valuables out of sight especially when you leave your car. Any loss or theft should be reported at once to the nearest *commissariat de police* or *gendarmerie* (see POLICE).

I want to report a theft.	**Je veux signaler un vol.**
My ticket/wallet/passport has been stolen.	**On a volé mon billet/portefeuille/passeport.**

D   **DRIVING IN FRANCE**

Entering France: To take your car into France you will need:

International Driving Licence or your national driving licence	Car registration papers	Green Card (an extension to your regular insurance making it valid for foreign countries) or other third-party insurance coverage valid for France.
	Nationality plate or sticker	

Note: You must have the nationality plate or sticker visible at the back of your car and a red warning triangle for use in emergencies. Drivers and passengers of cars fitted with seat belts are required by law to wear them. You will also need a blue zone parking disc *(disque de stationnement)*, obtainable from your motoring organization at home or, once in France, from a police station or tourist office.

Driving conditions: The rules are the same as elsewhere on the Continent — drive on the right, overtake on the left, yield right of way to all vehicles coming from the right, *even on roundabouts* unless otherwise indicated.

Speed limits now in force are 45 or 60 kilometres per hour (kph) in residential areas, 90 on the open road, 110 kph on dual carriageways (divided highways) and 130 on motorways (expressways). In case of precipitation, all limits are reduced by 10 kph.

The French style of driving can be terrifying if you're not used to it, with plenty of speed and daring overtaking. Stick to your own pace and keep a safe distance between yourself and the vehicle in front.

Road conditions: French roads are designated by an A, standing for *autoroute* (motorway); an N for national highways; a D for *départementale,* or regional roads; or a V for local roads *(chemins vicinaux)*. In recent years, road surfaces have been greatly improved. The *nationales,* or major highways, are good on the whole but often not as wide as they could be, especially at the time when most French people go on holiday: the 1st and 15th of July, the 1st and 15th of August and the 1st of September.

The motorways are excellent and owned by public companies which usually charge tolls according to vehicle size and distance travelled. All amenities (restaurants, toilets, service stations, etc.) are available, plus orange S.O.S. telephones every 2 kilometres.

Many tourists like to travel on secondary roads at a more leisurely pace with better views. Sometimes you'll find alternative routes *(itinéraires bis)* sign-posted along the way by emerald-green arrows.

Breakdowns: Towing and on-the-spot repairs can be made by local garages, and spare parts are readily available for European cars. It's wise to take out some form of internationally valid breakdown insurance before leaving home, and always ask for an estimate *before* undertaking repairs.

Traffic police: The *Garde Mobile* patrols the roads and motorways in cars or on powerful motorcycles. Always in pairs, they are courteous and helpful but extremely severe on lawbreakers and have authority to fine offenders on the spot.

Fuel and oil: Fuel is available in super (98 octane) and normal (90 octane). All grades of motor oil are on sale. It's usual to tip service-station attendants for any additional services rendered.

Fluid measures

D Distance

Road signs: Most road signs are the standard pictographs used throughout Europe, but you may encounter these written signs as well:

Accotements non stabilisés	Soft shoulders
Chaussée déformée	Bad road surface
Déviation	Diversion (detour)
Douane	Customs
Péage	Toll
Priorité à droite	Yield to traffic from right
Ralentir	Slow
Sauf riverains	Entry prohibited except for inhabitants of street
Serrez à droite/gauche	Keep right/left
Stationnement interdit	No parking

(international) driving licence	**permis de conduire (international)**
car registration papers	**carte grise**
Are we on the right road for...?	**Sommes-nous sur la route de...?**
Fill the tank, please	**Le plein, s'il vous plaît.**
regular/super	**normale/super**
Check the oil/tires/battery.	**Veuillez contrôler l'huile/ les pneus/la batterie**
I've had a breakdown.	**Ma voiture est en panne.**
There's been an accident.	**Il y a eu un accident.**

DRUGS. The possession, use and distribution of drugs are criminal offences. Prison sentences for offenders can be extremely severe, and suspects may have to wait a considerable time for trial—in jail.

E ELECTRIC CURRENT.

220-volt, 50-cycle A.C. is now almost universal, though 110 volts may still be encountered. British and American visitors using electric appliances should remember to buy a Continental adaptor plug before leaving home. They can also be bought in some electric supply shops *(magasins d'électricité)* or *drogueries.*

What's the voltage—110 or 220?	**Quel est le voltage – cent dix ou deux cent vingt?**
an adaptor plug/a battery	**une prise de raccordement/une pile**

112

EMERGENCIES *(urgence)*. For real emergencies you can get assistance anywhere in France by dialling the number 17 for the police *(Police-Secours)*; call number 18 for the fire brigade *(pompiers)* which also comes for such emergencies as drowning. For less pressing problems, see separate entries in this section such as CONSULATES, MEDICAL CARE, POLICE, etc.

Though we hope you'll never need them, here are a few key words you might like to learn in advance:

Careful!	**Attention!**
Fire!	**Au feu!**
Help!	**Au secours!**
Police!	**Police!**
Stop, thief!	**Au voleur!**
Can you help me?	**Pouvez-vous m'aider?**

ENTRY FORMALITIES and CUSTOMS *(douane)*. Most visitors need only a valid passport — no visa — to enter France. (British subjects can even enter on the simplified Visitor's Card.) Though European and North American residents are not subject to any health requirements, visitors from further afield should check with their travel agents before departure.

The following chart shows what main duty-free items you may take into France and, when returning home, into your own country:

Into:	Cigarettes		Cigars		Tobacco	Spirits		Wine
France[1])	400	or	100	or	500 g.	1 l.	and	2 l.
France[2])	200	or	50	or	250 g.	1 l.	and	2 l.
Canada	200	and	50	and	900 g.	1.1 l.	or	1.1 l.
Eire	200	or	50	or	250 g.	1 l.	and	2 l.
U.K.	200	or	50	or	250 g.	1 l.	and	2 l.
U.S.A.	200	and	100	and	1,350 g.	1 l.	or	1 l.

[1]) Visitors arriving from outside Europe
[2]) Visitors arriving from E.E.C. countries with duty-free items

E **Currency restrictions:** There's no limit on the importation of foreign currencies or traveller's cheques, but you may not leave the country with more than 5,000 French francs or the equivalent in foreign currency. If you plan to bring more than this sum in your own currency, you must establish a declaration on entry to enable you to re-export the same amount without trouble.

I've nothing to declare.	**Je n'ai rien à déclarer.**
It's for my own use.	**C'est pour mon usage personnel.**

G **GUIDES and INTERPRETERS*** *(guide; interprète)*. Local *syndicats d'initiative* (see TOURIST INFORMATION OFFICES) can supply or direct you to qualified official guides and interpreters if you want a personally conducted tour or any linguistic assistance. Guides engaged for a whole day should be offered lunch.

Bus companies from Nice and Cannes also offer many guided tours. It's customary to tip the guide.

We'd like an English-speaking guide.	**Nous aimerions un guide parlant anglais.**
I need an English interpreter.	**J'ai besoin d'un interprète anglais.**

H **HAIRDRESSERS* and BARBERS** *(coiffeur)*. Prices vary widely according to the class of establishment, but rates are often displayed in the window.

Tipping: Most establishments include *service* in the price, but it's customary to give a little something to the person who washes your hair, and a small tip to the stylist.

haircut	**coupe**
simple cut	**coupe simple**
shampoo and set	**shampooing et mise en plis**
blow-dry	**un brushing**
a colour chart	**un nuancier**
a colour rinse/hair-dye	**un rinçage/une teinture**
Not too much off (here).	**Pas trop court (ici).**
A little more off (here).	**Un peu plus court (ici).**

HITCH-HIKING *(auto-stop)*. This is permitted everywhere except on motorways. If you do hitch-hike, it's always wiser to go in pairs.

Can you give us a lift to...?   **Pouvez-vous nous emmener à...?**

HOTELS and ACCOMMODATION* *(hôtel; logement)*. See also CAMPING and YOUTH HOSTELS. France offers a huge variety of hotel accommodation to suit every taste and pocket.

Hotels are officially classified into five categories by the Commissariat Central du Tourisme. Room prices, fixed according to amenities, size and to the hotel's star rating, must be posted visibly at reception desks and behind each room door. Hotels marked *NN (Nouvelles Normes)* have recently been reclassified and correspond to current standards of comfort.

Note: Hôtel de Ville is not a hotel, but the town hall.

Other accommodation: This can run from the relatively modest *gîte* and *logis de France* to luxurious settings like the *château-hôtel* and *relais de campagne,* where prices can be very high.

House rental: Tourist offices can recommend agencies with complete lists of available houses and apartments to let. In full season, you should book well ahead.

a double/single room with/without bath	**une chambre à deux lits/à un lit avec/sans bains**
What's the rate per night?	**Quel est le prix pour une nuit?**
Must I take meals?	**Est-ce que la pension est obligatoire?**
I'm looking for a flat to rent for a month.	**Je cherche un appartement à louer pour un mois.**

LANGUAGE. Real southerners have a charming, droll accent, drawing out their syllables in a way you don't hear elsewhere. The usual nasal French "en" ending becomes a hard "ng" *(chien* sounds like *chieng)*.

In addition, you'll hear all sorts of rolling, vaguely Italianate dialects, especially Niçois and Monegasque. See also the box on page 14.

The Berlitz phrase book FRENCH FOR TRAVELLERS covers almost all situations you're likely to encounter in your travels in France. In addition, the Berlitz French-English/English-French pocket dictionary contains a 12,500 word glossary of each language, plus a menu-reader supplement.

Good morning/Good afternoon	**Bonjour**
Good afternoon/Good evening	**Bonsoir**
Please	**S'il vous plaît**
Thank you	**Merci**
You're welcome	**Je vous en prie**
Goodbye	**Au revoir**

L

LAUNDRY and DRY-CLEANING *(blanchisserie; teinturerie; nettoyage à sec)*. You'll still see some women in the Midi beating their laundry against the stone in the public fountain *lavoirs*. But modern facilities are growing fast.

If your hotel will not take care of laundry or cleaning, you can have clothes cleaned quickly and cheaply in chain dry-cleaners (not recommended, however, for fragile fabrics or difficult spots). Better care takes longer and is more expensive; prices vary according to fabric and cut.

When will it be ready?	**Quand est-ce que ce sera prêt?**
I must have it tomorrow morning.	**Il me le faut pour demain matin.**

LOST PROPERTY *(objets trouvés)*; **LOST CHILDREN.** Check first at your hotel desk and if you have no success there report the loss to the nearest *commissariat de police* or *gendarmerie* (see Police).

Restaurant and café personnel are quite honest about keeping objects forgotten or lost until the owner reclaims them, or in the case of wallets, turning them over to the police.

If you lose a child, you'll find people very helpful. It should be reported to any policeman *(agent de police)* on duty or the nearest *commissariat* or *gendarmerie*. In any case, don't let young children out of your sight in crowded places.

I've lost my child/wallet/handbag/passport.	**J'ai perdu mon enfant/portefeuille/sac/passeport.**

M

MAPS *(carte; plan)*. Various detailed topographical and road maps exist for motorists and hikers. Particularly useful is Michelin's No. 84, and the detailed map of the Alpes-Maritimes, No. 195. Falk-Verlag, who provided the maps for this guide, publishes a map of France.

Do you have a map of the city/of the region?	**Avez-vous un plan de la ville/une carte de la région?**

MEDICAL CARE. See also Emergencies. To be at ease, make sure your health insurance policy covers any illness or accident while on holiday. If not, ask your insurance representative, automobile association or travel agent for details of special travel insurance.

You'll find well-trained doctors and specialists in the south of France. If you're taken ill or have a toothache, consult your hotel receptionist, who can probably recommend an English-speaking doctor or dentist.

Visitors from EEC countries with corresponding health insurance facilities are entitled to medical and hospital treatment under the French social security system. Before leaving home, make sure you find out about the appropriate form(s) required to obtain this benefit in case of need. Doctors who belong to the French social security system *(médecins conventionnés)* charge the minimum.

Chemists' *(pharmacie)* with green crosses are helpful in dealing with minor ailments or in finding a nurse *(infirmière)* if you need injections or other special care.

Health *(santé)*. The "tourist's complaint" that hits many travellers is not due to drinking tap water, which is safe in towns all over France. Fatigue, too much sun, change of diet and over-indulgence are the main causes of most minor complaints. Be careful about over-eating and, especially, drinking. French mineral water is a good thirst quencher and helps to digest meals. Serious gastro-intestinal problems lasting more than a day or two should be looked after by a doctor.

Where's the chemist on duty?	**Où est la pharmacie de garde?**
I need a doctor.	**Il me faut un médecin.**
a dentist	**un dentiste**
an upset stomach	**mal à l'estomac**
a fever	**de la fièvre**
sunburn	**un coup de soleil**
I've a pain here.	**J'ai mal ici.**

MEETING PEOPLE. See also COURTESIES. The French Riviera has been for many years a very cosmopolitan and popular resort area, not only for foreigners but for the northern French themselves. Something of a blasé attitude towards tourists may be met with in the over-frequented spots, while off the beaten track spontaneous warmth and kindness are as alive as ever. This natural friendliness on the part of girls, however, should not be taken as an invitation to forego the normal approach procedures. Do not consider a topless beauty an easy mark; she may prefer to stay alone or with her companions. As for French men, you will find them slightly less brash than other southern Europeans.

MONEY MATTERS

Currency *(monnaie)*. For currency restrictions, see ENTRY FORMALITIES and CUSTOMS. The *franc*, France's monetary unit (abbreviated F or FF) is divided into 100 *centimes*. Current coins include 5-, 10-, 20- and 50-

M centime pieces as well as 1-, 2-, 5- and 10-franc pieces. Banknotes come in denominations of 20, 50, 100, 200 and 500 francs.

Many French people still like to express prices in "old" francs *(anciens francs)* — although the system changed 20 years ago: 100 of them equal 1 "new" franc. In shops, however, only new francs are referred to.

Banks and Currency-Exchange Offices *(banques; bureau de change)*. Hours may vary, but most banks are open Monday to Friday from 8.30 or 9.30 a.m. to noon and 1.30 to 5 p.m. Some currency-exchange offices operate on Saturdays as well. At Monte Carlo, a *bureau de change* opposite the Casino is open every day.

Your hotel will usually change currency or traveller's cheques into francs, but the rate is not favourable—nor is it in shops and casinos where traveller's cheques are often accepted. Always take your passport along when you go to change money.

Credit Cards *(carte de crédit)*. Most hotels, smarter restaurants, some boutiques, car-hire firms and tourist-related businesses in towns accept certain credit cards.

Traveller's cheques *(chèque de voyage)*. Hotels, travel agents and many shops accept them, although the exchange rate is invariably better at a bank. Don't forget to take your passport when going to cash a traveller's cheque. Eurocheques are also accepted.

Prices *(prix)*. The cost of living on the Riviera is generally high, but it is possible to have a good time on a budget if you choose carefully. (The further you get away from the coast, the more likely you are to find reasonably priced hotels and restaurants.)

Official prices are always posted prominently in public establishments, including cafés, bars, hotels and restaurants.

Could you give me some (small) change?	**Pouvez-vous me donner de la (petite) monnaie?**
I want to change some pounds/dollars.	**Je voudrais changer des livres sterling/des dollars.**
Do you accept traveller's cheques?	**Acceptez-vous les chèques de voyage?**
Can I pay with this credit card?	**Puis-je payer avec cette carte de crédit?**

N NEWSPAPERS and MAGAZINES *(journal; revue)*. In addition to French national and local papers, most towns also have British newspapers for sale and the Paris-based *International Herald Tribune*, usually on publication day.

Magazines in many languages are available at larger news-stands.

Have you any English-language newspapers?	**Avez-vous des journaux en anglais?**

PETS *(animal domestique)*. If you want to bring your pet dog or cat along, you'll need a health and rabies inoculation certificate for the animal to enter the country. Many hotels and restaurants allow pets, but check first.

PHOTOGRAPHY *(photographie)*. The coast is a photographer's dream, with plenty of light, varied scenery and colours of every intensity from soft pastel shades to the most vibrant hues. Certain museums will give you permission to photograph inside.

All popular film makes and sizes are available in France. Rapid development is possible, but quite expensive.

I'd like a film for this camera.	**J'aimerais un film pour cet appareil.**
a black-and-white film	**un film noir et blanc**
a film for colour prints	**un film couleurs**
a colour-slide film	**un film de diapositives**
How long will it take to develop this film?	**Combien de temps faut-il pour développer ce film?**
Can I take a picture of you?	**Puis-je vous prendre en photo?**

POLICE *(police)*. In cities and larger towns you'll see the blue-uniformed *police municipale;* they are the local police force who keep order, investigate crime and direct traffic. Outside of the main towns are the *gendarmes*—they wear blue trousers and black jackets with white belts and are also responsible for traffic and crime investigation.

The C.R.S. police *(Compagnies Républicaines de Sécurité)* are a national security force responsible to the Ministry of the Interior and are called in for emergencies and special occasions. The *Garde Mobile,* or *Police de la Route,* patrol the roads.

In case of need, dial 17 anywhere in France for police help.

Where's the nearest police station?	**Où est le poste de police le plus proche?**

P **PUBLIC HOLIDAYS** *(jours férié)*

January 1	*Jour de l'An*	New Year's Day
May 1	*Fête du Travail*	Labour Day
May 8	*Fête de la Libération*	Victory Day (1945)
July 14	*Fête Nationale*	Bastille Day
August 15	*Assomption*	Assumption
November 1	*Toussaint*	All Saints' Day
November 11	*Anniversaire* *de l'Armistice*	Armistice Day
December 25	*Noël*	Christmas Day
Movable dates:	*Lundi de Pâques*	Easter Monday
	Ascension	Ascension
	Lundi de Pentecôte	Whit Monday

These are the national French holidays. See page 81 for details of local celebrations and events.

PUBLIC TRANSPORT

Buses *(autobus, autocar)*. Larger towns and cities like Cannes, Nice, Toulon and Monte Carlo have urban bus services — a particularly good way to get around. Inter-city bus services all along the coast and into the hinterland are efficient, comfortable, inexpensive and fairly frequent.

Taxis★ *(taxi)*. Taxis are clearly marked and available in all the larger towns. If the cab is unmetered, or you have a fair distance to go, ask the fare beforehand.

Trains *(train)*. The French National Railways *(S.N.C.F.)* run efficient, punctual train services. At least three trains a day go from Paris' Gare de Lyon directly to the Côte d'Azur. The best are the crack luxury day train, the *Mistral,* and the equally comfortable night train, the *Train Bleu,* both famous for excellent accommodation and restaurant service.

Trains are also a good way of getting around the coast quickly and cheaply in the height of summer traffic. The train ride from Menton to Nice, for example, lasts half an hour; by car or bus the same trip may take you an hour or more.

S.N.C.F. offer various categories of ticket, like Billet Touristique, Billet de Groupes, Billet de Famille, France-Vacances, etc. Inquire at the nearest tourist office or railway information counter. Eurailpasses and **120** Inter-rail cards are valid in France (see p. 101).

When's the next bus/train to...?	**Quand part le prochain bus/ train pour...?**
When's the best train to...?	**A quelle heure part le meilleur train pour...?**
single (one-way)	**aller simple**
return (round-trip)	**aller et retour**
first/second class	**première/deuxième classe**
I'd like to make seat reservations.	**J'aimerais réserver des places.**

RADIO and TV *(radio; télévision)*. There are three colour TV channels in France. Some hotels have television lounges; a few have TV in the rooms. All programmes (except for a few late films) are in French. Monte Carlo television can also be picked up in most places along the coast.

You can easily tune in to BBC programmes on either short- or medium-wave radios. In summer the French radio broadcasts news and information in English. Local newspapers have the details. Radio Nova transmits in English all day on 101.2 FM.

RELIGIOUS SERVICES. France is a predominantly Roman Catholic country. Ask your hotel receptionist or the local tourist office for information about the location and times of services in English. There are English-speaking Protestant churches and synagogues in Antibes, Cannes, Menton, Monaco and Nice. Non-Catholic services are called *cultes*.

| Where is the Protestant church/ synagogue? | **Où se trouve l'église protestante/ la synagogue?** |
| What time is mass/the service? | **A quelle heure est la messe/ le culte?** |

TIME DIFFERENCES. France follows Greenwich Mean Time + 1, and in spring the clocks are put forward one hour. If your country does the same, the time difference remains constant for most of the year.

Los Angeles	Chicago	New York	London	**Nice**
3 a.m.	5 a.m.	6 a.m.	11 a.m.	**noon**

| What time is it? | **Quelle heure est-il?** |

T **TIPPING.** A 10 to 15% service charge is generally included automatically in hotel and restaurant bills. Rounding off the overall bill helps round off friendships with waiters, too. It is also in order to hand the bellboys, doormen, filling station attendants, etc., a coin or two for their service.

The chart below gives some suggestions as to what to leave.

Hairdresser/Barber	15% (gen. incl.)
Hotel maid, per week	10–15 F
Lavatory attendant	1–2 F
Porter, per bag	3 F
Taxi driver	10–15%
Tourist guide	10%
Waiter	5–10% (optional)

TOILETS *(toilettes).* Clean public conveniences are still not all that common in France, and the stand-up toilet facilities can be rather harrowing. If there is no light-switch, the light will usually go on when you lock the door. Three-star W.C.'s do exist, mostly in better hotels and restaurants.

Café facilities are generally free, but you should order at least a coffee if you use the toilet. A saucer with small change on it means that a tip is expected. The women's toilets may be marked *Dames;* the men's either *Messieurs* or *Hommes.*

Where are the toilets, please? **Où sont les toilettes, s'il vous plaît?**

TOURIST INFORMATION OFFICES *(office du tourisme).* French national tourist offices can help you plan your holiday and will supply you with a wide range of colourful, informative brochures and maps.

Some addresses:

Canada: 1840 Ouest, rue Sherbrooke, Montreal H3H 1E4, P.Q.; tel.: (514) 931-3855
372 Bay St., Suite 610, Toronto M5H 2W9, Ont.; tel.: (416) 361-1605

122 **United Kingdom:** 178, Piccadilly, London W1V OAL; tel.: (01) 491-7622

U.S.A. 645 N. Michigan Ave., Suite 430, Chicago IL 60611; tel.: (312) 337-6301

9401 Wilshire Blvd., Room 840, Beverly Hills CA 90212; tel.: (213) 271-6665

610 5th Ave., New York NY 10020; tel.: (212) 757-1125

World Trade Centre 103, 2050 Stemmens Freeway, P.O. Box 58610 Dallas TX 75258; tel.: (214) 742-7011

On the spot:

Nice:	Gare Centrale, Avenue Thiers; tel.: (93) 87 07 07 airport (high season only)
Cannes:	Services de Tourisme, 50, La Croisette; tel.: (93) 39 24 53 (ask for the Office du Tourisme)
Monaco:	2a, Boulevard des Moulins; tel.: (93) 30 87 01
Marseilles:	4, Canebière; tel.: (91) 54 91 91

French Riviera Tourist Board – Comité Régional du Tourisme Riviera Côte d'Azur – 55, Promenade des Anglais, 06000 Nice; tel.: (93) 44 50 59

Local tourist information offices *(syndicat d'initiative)* are invaluable sources of information (from maps to hotel lists and other miscellaneous items) in all French towns. They are usually found near the town's centre and often have a branch at the railway station. Opening hours vary, but the general rule is 8.30 or 9 a.m. to noon and from 2 to 6 or 7 p.m., every day except Sunday.

Where's the tourist office, please? **Où est le syndicat d'initiative, s'il vous plaît?**

WATER *(eau)*. Tap water is safe throughout the country, except when marked *eau non potable* (not safe for drinking). A wide variety of mineral water can be found on sale everywhere.

a bottle of mineral water **une bouteille d'eau minérale**
  carbonated   **gazeuse**
  non-carbonated   **non gazeuse**
Is this drinking water? **Est-ce de l'eau potable?**

YOUTH HOSTELS *(auberge de jeunesse)*. Your national youth hostel association can give you all the details, or contact the

Fédération Unie des Auberges de Jeunesse, 6, rue Mesnil, 75116 Paris; tel. (1) 261 84 03.

DAYS OF THE WEEK

DAYS

Sunday	**dimanche**	Thursday	**jeudi**
Monday	**lundi**	Friday	**vendredi**
Tuesday	**mardi**	Saturday	**samedi**
Wednesday	**mercredi**		

MONTHS

MONTHS

January	**janvier**	July	**juillet**
February	**février**	August	**août**
March	**mars**	September	**septembre**
April	**avril**	October	**octobre**
May	**mai**	November	**novembre**
June	**juin**	December	**décembre**

NUMBERS

NUMBERS

0	**zéro**	19	**dix-neuf**
1	**un, une**	20	**vingt**
2	**deux**	21	**vingt et un**
3	**trois**	22	**vingt-deux**
4	**quatre**	23	**vingt-trois**
5	**cinq**	30	**trente**
6	**six**	40	**quarante**
7	**sept**	50	**cinquante**
8	**huit**	60	**soixante**
9	**neuf**	70	**soixante-dix**
10	**dix**	71	**soixante et onze**
11	**onze**	80	**quatre-vingts**
12	**douze**	90	**quatre-vingt-dix**
13	**treize**	100	**cent**
14	**quatorze**	101	**cent un**
15	**quinze**	126	**cent vingt-six**
16	**seize**	200	**deux cents**
17	**dix-sept**	300	**trois cents**
18	**dix-huit**	1000	**mille**

SOME USEFUL EXPRESSIONS

yes/no	**oui/non**
please/thank you	**s'il vous plaît/merci**
excuse me	**excusez-moi**
you're welcome	**je vous en prie**
where/when/how	**où/quand/comment**
how long/how far	**combien de temps/à quelle distance**
yesterday/today/tomorrow	**hier/aujourd'hui/demain**
day/week/month/year	**jour/semaine/mois/année**
left/right	**gauche/droite**
up/down	**en haut/en bas**
good/bad	**bon/mauvais**
big/small	**grand/petit**
cheap/expensive	**bon marché/cher**
hot/cold	**chaud/froid**
old/new	**vieux/neuf**
open/closed	**ouvert/fermé**
here/there	**ici/là**
free (vacant)/occupied	**libre/occupé**
early/late	**tôt/tard**
easy/difficult	**facile/difficile**

Does anyone here speak English?	**Y a-t-il quelqu'un ici qui parle anglais?**
What does this mean?	**Que signifie ceci?**
I don't understand.	**Je ne comprends pas.**
Please write it down.	**Ecrivez-le-moi, s'il vous plaît.**
Is there an admission charge?	**Faut-il payer pour entrer?**
Waiter/Waitress!	**Garçon/Mademoiselle!**
I'd like...	**J'aimerais...**
How much is that?	**C'est combien?**
Have you something less expensive?	**Avez-vous quelque chose de moins cher?**
What time is it?	**Quelle heure est-il?**
Help me please.	**Aidez-moi, s'il vous plaît.**

125

Index

An asterisk (*) next to a page number indicates a map reference. For sites and town names starting with an article (le, la, les, l') see the basic word. For index to Practical Information, see p. 104.

INDEX

127

INDEX

128